ETHICS
AND THE
SOCIOLOGY
OF MORALS

ETHICS
AND THE
SOCIOLOGY
OF MORALS

EMILE
DURKHEIM

Translated with an introduction
by Robert T. Hall

GREAT MINDS SERIES

PROMETHEUS BOOKS
Buffalo, New York

Published 1993 by Prometheus Books

97 96 95 94 93   5 4 3 2 1

Library of Congress Cataloging-in-Publication Data

Durkheim, Emile, 1858–1917.
    [Science positive de la morale en allemagne. English]
    Ethics and the sociology of morals / Emile Durkheim.
        p.   cm. — (Great minds series)
    Includes bibliographical references.
    ISBN 0-87975-845-7 (pbk)
    1. Ethics—Germany—History—19th century. 2. Social sciences and ethics. 3. Ethics, Modern—19th century. I. Title. II. Series.
BJ752.D8713   1993
303.3'72—dc20   93-5459
                                                                 CIP

Printed in the United States of America on acid-free paper.

Also Available in Prometheus's Great Minds Paperback Series

Charles Darwin
The Origin of Species

Michael Faraday
The Forces of Matter

Galileo Galilei
*Dialogues Concerning
Two New Sciences*

Edward Gibbon
On Christianity

Ernst Haeckel
The Riddle of the Universe

William Harvey
*On the Motion of the Heart
and Blood in Animals*

Herodotus
The History

Julian Huxley
Evolutionary Humanism

Thomas Henry Huxley
*Agnosticism and Christianity
and Other Essays*

Ernest Renan
The Life of Jesus

Adam Smith
Wealth of Nations

Andrew D. White
*A History of the Warfare of
Science with Theology in
Christendom*

See the back of this volume for a complete list of titles in Prometheus's Great Books in Philosophy and Great Minds series.

Contents

Preface

My purpose in presenting a translation of this early Durkheim article is a little more pointed than the idea of making available in English a neglected essay by a master of social thought. It is more specific in two ways. First, as I outline in the "Introduction," I believe that the essay is an important key to the programmatic orientation of Durkheim's thought—an orientation he called the science of moral facts, which I call simply the sociology of morals. Secondly, the essay presents a number of aspects of Durkheim's ethical theory which are of considerable interest in the light of current ethical theory. Together these dimensions of Durkheim's thought raise questions which I believe to be crucial to the development of social theory. Should the sociology of morals be considered a separate field within sociology? If so, how should it be related to philosophical ethics? How can social theory and research give an account of the moral dimension of society which is relevant to current ethical theory?

I wish to thank a number of people for their help: Mary Frye, my colleague at West Virginia State College, for her assistance with some of the sticky points of the translation; the late Donald T. Hartman, who was Campus Executive Officer at Penn State DuBois Campus, for his comments and editorial advice; Paul Kurtz of Prometheus Books for his special interest in the subject; Mary Lucas for secretarial help; and my wife, Mary Kay Buchmelter, for her loving support and encouragement.

Introduction

When he completed his formal education in 1882 at the École Normale Supérieure, Emile Durkheim became a professor of philosophy first at the Lycée de Puy, then at Sens, then at Saint-Quentin. In 1885 he was awarded a scholarship by the Ministry of Public Instruction to visit various German universities for the purpose of reviewing current developments in philosophy and the social sciences. Durkheim reported his findings in two articles, "La Philosophie dans les universités allemandes," published in the *Revue Internationale de l'Enseignement,*[1] and the article translated here, "La Science positive de la morale en Allemagne," published in the *Revue Philosophique.*[2] The former was a rather straightforward account of current philosophical doctrines and teaching. The latter, however, which I have entitled "Ethics and the Sociology of Morals," actually laid the foundation for Durkheim's future work. It was more than a review of current thought; it was a manifesto of sorts—a proclamation that ethics needed to be liberated from its philosophical bondage and developed as a distinct branch of sociology. "The conclusion of this whole study," Durkheim said near the end, "is that the science of morality is just in the process of being born."[3] Written, as it was, when Durkheim was charting the course of his own research, it provides a unique key to the

---

1. 1887, Vol. XIII, pp. 313–38, 423–40.
2. 1887, Vol. XXIV, pp. 33–58, 113–42, 275–84.
3. Quotations without reference here are to the article above.

interpretation of his later work—a programmatic statement of his sociology.

DURKHEIM'S SOCIOLOGY OF MORALS PROGRAM

The notion that the sociology of morals was the central programmatic theme of Durkheim's thought requires some elaboration. First, it is not intended as a claim that this was Durkheim's most important concept or theory. Durkheim's major concepts (collective consciousness, anomie, organic solidarity, etc.) and theories (suicide, social solidarity, religion, etc.) are important contributions to sociology in their own right. The fact that they retain so much of their value today is testimony enough to their significance.

To say that the central programmatic theme of Durkheim's thought was his notion of a sociology of morals is to say that this was the field of study or research tradition within which he developed the concepts and theories for which he is remembered. It is a statement of "what Durkheim thought he was doing" when he developed his major concepts and theories and indicates, in an important way, how these concepts and theories fit together.[4] Just as one might characterize Marx as a conflict theorist and indicate that the field of study from which he developed a general social theory was political economy, so Durkheim might be characterized as a moral theorist or sociologist of morals whose general social theory might be regarded as a moral perspective.

While a research program or tradition is not the same as a concept or theory, neither is it a paradigm in the sense of a set of methodological principles or a theory of explanation. Durkheim's understanding of sociological explanation in terms of its basic

---

4. On the notion of a "research tradition" see Larry Laudan, *Progress and Its Problems: Toward a Theory of Scientific Growth,* 1977, Berkeley, Calif.: University of California Press; on the use of this notion for the interpretation of Durkheim's thought see Robert T. Hall, *Emile Durkheim: Ethics and the Sociology of Morals,* 1987, New York: Greenwood Press, Chapter 15.

elements (social facts) and methodology (historical, causal, and functional explanation) are well known. Durkheim described his own theory of sociological explanation in *The Rules of Sociological Method*.[5] A research tradition requires certain basic commitments concerning the nature of scientific explanation, but it also employs the methodology and theory of explanation it presupposes in a particular area of interest. The term 'paradigm,' therefore, implies too much. It is not Durkheim's philosophy of science that is at issue here; it is his area of interest and the collection of interlocking concepts and theories that constitute this area. Durkheim believed that any adequate explanation of a society must include an account of the evolution, the nature and the function of the moral norms and beliefs of the members of that society. The designation he used for this branch of sociology was the "science of moral facts" or what we might now call the sociology of morals.

The sociology of morals program is easily overlooked in Durkheim's writings because we do not now commonly identify the sociology of morals as a distinct research field within sociology. A number of Durkheim's followers and a few later theorists like Jean Piaget saw themselves as continuing his efforts, but the field never developed as a unified body of research. It was especially unattractive to English-speaking social theorists for a number of reasons: it was too philosophical in its definition of 'morality' and consequently too weak empirically; it was too historical in its methodology to fit in with the 'scientific' image sociologists wanted to present; and it was politically too conservative in its identification of morality with social solidarity. The major theoretical alternatives that developed by the middle of the twentieth century had no need of a sociology of morals. Conflict theorists held that basic values were primarily economic and therefore unproblematic. Functional theorists tended to assume that values were basically constant and therefore equally unproblematic. Alvin Gouldner described the plight of the sociology of morals as a "structural lacuna" in twentieth century social theory:

---

5. 1982, New York: The Free Press.

Despite the fact that Academic Sociology, beginning with Sociological Positivism, had hailed the significance of shared moral values, despite the fact that Emile Durkheim had called for and promised to create such a sociology of morals, and despite the fact that a concern with moral values was central to Max Weber's sociology of religion as well as to Talcott Parsons' "voluntaristic" theory, there still remains no concentration of scholarship that might be called a "sociology of moral values" and would correspond in cumulative development to specialized areas, such as the study of social stratification, role analysis, political sociology, let alone to criminology or to family studies. . . . Structurally, then, Academic Sociology is characterized both by the importance it attributes to values and by its failure to develop—in its characteristic manner which transforms almost everything into a specialization—a distinctive sociology of moral values.[6]

The extent to which Durkheim was aware of the development of a sociology of morals in the work of Wilhelm Wundt and others before his trip to Germany is undocumented. It is clear, however, that the lectures he attended and his reading in Germany struck an important note. What he saw as a new school of moral theorists which attempted to approach the subject "as a special science with its own methods and principles" stood in sharp contrast to the perspective of the social philosophers with whom he had studied in France. It held out, for him, the possibility of a new discipline—one which would investigate morality from a sociological perspective. The study was to be empirical and, for the most part, historical. It would trace the evolution of moral ideas, but would involve causal and functional explanations as well. The sociology of morals, Durkheim wrote,

is not an applied or derived science, but an autonomous one. It has its own object of investigation, just as the physicist studies physical facts or the biologist biological facts, and it studies these using the same methods. Its facts consist of mores, customs, legal

---

6. *The Coming Crisis of Western Sociology,* 1971, New York: Avon Books, pp. 140–41.

prescriptions, and economic phenomena in so far as they become the object of legal prescriptions. It observes them, analyzes them, compares them, and raises itself progressively toward laws which explain them.

Durkheim had, in fact, the dual purpose of developing first a sociological study of morality and then, based upon this study, a new ethical theory. I will comment below on Durkheim's ethical theory and his view of the relationship between the sociology of morals and ethics. In my account of Durkheim's sociology of morals in this section, however, I have in mind only his approach to morality as a field of study for sociology. In general, I use the terms 'morality' and 'moral theorist' for the sociology of morals and reserve the terms 'ethics' and 'moral philosopher' for the philosophical perspective.

Durkheim referred to the sociology of morals as his "chosen field" of study in his inaugural lecture at Bordeaux where he was appointed *chargé de cours* of social science and pedagogy at the Faculty of Letters in 1887. His extensive references to the German theorists mentioned in his article indicates the continuity of his thought on this matter and demonstrates the importance of the article as a programmatic statement. In the outline of the social sciences he presented, the second major division (following social psychology and preceding the sociology of law and economics as the third and fourth divisions) was the sociology of morals. "Of all the aspects of sociology," he said, "morality is the one to which I am attracted by my own preference and which holds my attention before all else." This was no offhand remark; Durkheim was quite clearly charting the specific course of his future work. "My predominant concern," he said, "is to limit and circumscribe as much as possible the extent of my research, for I am quite convinced that it is necessary for sociology to put an end to the era of generalities."[7]

---

7. "Cours de science sociale: leçon d'ouverture," in *La Science sociale et l'action,* Paris: 1970, PUF, pp. 105–106; translated in Mark Traugott, ed., *Emile Durkheim on Institutional Analysis,* 1978, Chicago: The University of Chicago Press.

Durkheim's first major work, *The Division of Labor,* was, as he himself conceived it, a study in the sociology of morals. "This book," he wrote in the "Preface" to the first edition, "is preeminently an attempt to treat the facts of the moral life according to the methods of the positive sciences." He then drew a clear distinction between his concept of a sociology of morals and the 'scientific method' adopted by moral philosophers.

> A use has been made of this method, that distorts its meaning, and which we oppose. The moralists who deduce their doctrines, not from some *a priori* principle, but from some propositions borrowed from one of the positive sciences like biology, psychology, sociology, call their ethics scientific. We do not propose to follow this method. We do not wish to extract ethics from science, but to establish the science of ethics, which is quite different. Moral facts are phenomena like others; they consist of rules of action recognizable by certain distinctive characteristics. It must, then, be possible to observe them, describe them, classify them, and look for the laws explaining them.[8]

Durkheim's second major work, *Suicide,* was conceived as another contribution to his sociology of morals program. As a "moral statistic," suicide rates were important indicators of the nature and degree of moral solidarity in a society—"an echo of the moral state of society."[9] Durkheim's explanation of suicide was itself a sociology of morals explanation: "The maladjustment from which we suffer," he wrote in his conclusion,

> does not exist because the objective causes of suffering have increased in number or intensity; it bears witness not to a greater economic poverty, but to an alarming poverty of morality. . . . [B]y calling the evil of which the abnormal increase in suicides is symptomatic a moral evil, we are far from thinking to reduce it to some superficial ill which may be conjured away by soft words. On the contrary, the change in moral temperament thus

---

8. *The Division of Labor in Society,* 1933, New York: The Free Press, p. 32.

9. Emile Durkheim, *Suicide,* 1951, New York: The Free Press, p. 300.

betrayed bears witness to a profound change in our social structure. To cure the one, therefore, the other must be reformed.[10]

Durkheim pursued the sociology of morals program actively in his lectures, first at Bordeaux, then at Paris. In a series of lectures published in 1950 under the title *Professional Ethics and Civic Morals,* he offered a brief outline of the field:

> The science of morals and rights should be based on the study of moral and juridical facts. These facts consist of rules of conduct that have received sanction. The problems to be solved in this field of study are: (1) How these rules were established in the course of time: that is, what were the causes that gave rise to them and the useful ends they serve. (2) The way in which they operate in society; that is, how they are applied to individuals.[11]

The French title of this work, taken from Durkheim's lectures, *Leçons de sociologie: Physique des moeurs et du droit,* itself indicates the research tradition Durkheim had in mind. The subtitle could be translated "The Nature of Moral Norms and Law," or even "The Natural History of Moral Norms and Law." Durkheim's student and later collaborator, Marcel Mauss, was quite clear about Durkheim's comprehensive programmatic intent in these lectures. Durkheim had divided the subject into two parts, according to Mauss: (1) social morality, which consisted of the study of the obligations that all people have to one another and to society in general, and (2) the morality of special social groups, which included the study of obligations that arise from one's participation in social institutions and organizations such as the family or professional groups. Mauss said that in lectures such as these, "Durkheim had established the 'Sociology of Morals' "—a science "of which he not only conceived the idea, but began to fill in the outline."[12]

---

10. Durkheim, *Suicide,* pp. 386–87.

11. Emile Durkheim, *Professional Ethics and Civic Morals,* 1958, Glencoe, Ill.: The Free Press, p. 1.

12. Marcel Mauss, *Oeuvres,* 1968–69, Paris: PUF, Vol. 3, p. 480.

Durkheim's most theoretical analysis of the nature of morality appears in a volume which is not widely read by sociologists today and is seldom recognized for its contribution to his research program—his lectures on *Moral Education.* Here again he was very clear about the programmatic nature of his efforts. "The fact is," he said, "a science has been established, which is still now making its debut, but which attempts to treat the phenomena of the moral life as natural phenomena."[13] Durkheim's purpose in these lectures was to show that public (i.e., secular) education could and should include moral education based not upon religion, but upon a sociological study of the nature of the existing social morality. The analytical part of this work that is especially important to Durkheim's sociology of morals program is his attempt to distinguish moral norms, moral ideals, and moral motives as elements of the complex phenomenon of morality.[14]

In his work on the sociological journal *L'Année Sociologique,* Durkheim referred again and again to his sociology of morals program. He began a review of Lucien Lévy-Bruhl's *Ethics and Moral Science,* for example, with the following statement: "One will find in this work, analyzed and demonstrated with rare vigor, the very idea that is basic to everything we are doing here [i.e., in Durkheim's own research program], namely that there is a positive science of moral acts, and that it is on this science that the moralists' practical speculation must rely."[15] Of the six sections of *L'Année* Durkheim himself chose to edit the division that included the sociology of morals.

In a later review Durkheim seemed especially annoyed that the authors in question had not recognized the extent to which his sociology of morals program had already been developed in his own books and lectures.

---

13. Emile Durkheim, *L'Education morale,* 1974, Paris: PUF, p. 5; see *Moral Education,* 1973, New York: The Free Press, p. 5.

14. See Hall, *Emile Durkheim,* Chapters 4, 5, and 6.

15. Yash Nandan, ed., *Emile Durkheim: Contributions to* L'Année Sociologique, 1980, New York: The Free Press, p. 130.

All these authors deal with the method we are practicing, but in a completely abstract manner, as if it were still only a project, as if it had never been applied. Nonetheless, if the science of moral facts, such as we conceive it, is still in its rudimentary stage, it does not mean that it is not yet born; and there is some exaggeration and injustice done to us by speaking of its mere possibility—which will perhaps be realized, however, in an indeterminate future. Already our *Division of Labor* has been presented as being "first and foremost an effort to deal with the facts of moral life in accordance with the method of the positive sciences" [preface to the first edition]. Our book *Suicide*, all the *Mémoires* we have published here, all the analyses and discussions of books concerning juridic and moral sociology that we publish each year in *L'Année*, come from the same premises.[16]

An especially significant statement of the programmatic nature of Durkheim's work dates from 1906, almost twenty years after his article on the sociology of morals in Germany. It was an address he gave to the French Philosophical Society entitled "The Determination of Moral Fact." Durkheim began by distinguishing the sociology of morals (which he called the "explanation" of morality) from ethics (the "evaluation" of morality) and indicated that his major concern was the former. Any science, he said, must begin with a precise demarcation of the subject—the "determination of moral fact." Morality, he said, encompasses all those social norms and rules which are accompanied by sanctions giving them a certain coercive power. The second aspect of morality is what Durkheim called the "desirability" of the actions in question or what we would now call moral motivation. He then moved from the defining characteristics to the explanation of morality in terms of (1) its causes and (2) its social functions. In the course of the discussion Durkheim brought out what amounts to a third characteristic of morality, its ideal nature. The ideal aspect of morality, he said, was central to his concept of society.

---

16. Nandan, *Emile Durkheim: Contributions to* L'Année Sociologique, pp. 137–38.

> Society . . . is above all a composition of ideas, beliefs and sentiments of all sorts which realize themselves through individuals. Foremost of these ideas is the moral ideal which is its principle *raison d'être*.[17]

The concluding paragraph of this talk (before Durkheim responded to questions) makes it quite clear that he conceived the sociology of morals as the research program to which he had dedicated his life: "Such then—as far as it can be outlined in the course of a lecture—is the general conception of moral facts to which research on this subject for a little over twenty years has led me."[18]

In response to questions, Durkheim specified what he meant by the sociology of morals in more detail and distinguished it from other branches of sociology.

> The science of which I speak is not general sociology, and I am not trying to say that research into social structures and political and economic systems will produce deductions as to the moral system. . . . In order to understand morality we must proceed from the moral data of the present and the past. Certainly this science of moral facts is, I am convinced, a sociological science, but it is a very particular branch of sociology. . . . Moral facts are related to other social facts . . . , but they form, in the society, a distinct sphere.[19]

There is also an interesting footnote in the second section of Durkheim's answers to questions. In what amounts to an allusion to the article translated here, Durkheim mentioned that he had borrowed part of his analysis of morality from Wilhelm Wundt's three-volume work, *Ethics*.[20] An analysis of Wundt's work constitutes almost half of the article. Durkheim was, in fact, criticized for borrowing so much from Wundt.

Durkheim's work on religion ought to be mentioned here as

---

17. Emile Durkheim, *Sociology and Philosophy,* 1953, Glencoe, Ill.: The Free Press, p. 59.

18. Ibid., p. 62.

19. Ibid., pp. 71–71.

20. Ibid., p. 49.

well. *The Elementary Forms of the Religious life,* together with Durkheim's *Primitive Classifications* (with Marcel Mauss) and his lectures on Pragmatism constitute a study of human knowledge which was a parallel to his study of morality—a sociology of knowledge related to his sociology of morals. "If society is to thrive," he concluded, "there is need not only of a sufficient moral conformity, but also of a minimal logical conformity."[21]

Finally, Durkheim's very last essay must be mentioned because it shows that he still had his plan for a sociology of morals in mind at the end of his life. When he died in 1917, Durkheim had just begun to edit the lectures he had given at the Sorbonne with the intent of publishing them in a three-volume work entitled *La Morale.* The work would have included his lectures on civic and professional morality,[22] his work on the family (which was eventually lost), and, I believe, much of the theoretical analysis included in his lectures on *Moral Education* which had not been published.

Durkheim only completed a rough draft of the "Introduction" to this work. It contains, however, an explicit statement of the programmatic nature of his understanding of the sociology of morals.

> The name we now give to this science is the 'science or natural philosophy of social norms' [*science ou physique des moeurs*]. The word '*moeurs*' denotes in our view that morality [*morale*] which men actually observe throughout history and which is vested with the authority of tradition, as contrasted with what the moralist conceives as the morality of the future. . . . It deals with moral phenomena, with moral reality, as it appears to observation, whether in the present or in the past, just as physics or physiology deals with the study of facts.

> The work of which we now offer the first volume is intended to provide a complete survey of the current state of this science, to describe therefore and to explain to the best of our knowledge

---

21. Emile Durkheim, *The Elementary Forms of the Religious Life: A Study in Religious Sociology,* 1965, New York: The Free Press, p. 30.
22. Later published as *Professional Ethics and Civic Morals.*

the principal facts of the moral life, and to draw from these theoretical studies the practical conclusions implicit in them.[23]

In addition to the references in his major works, therefore, we have three explicit statements of Durkheim's programmatic concept of the sociology of morals as a specific research field within sociology: his "Introduction to *La Morale*" written in 1917 as the outline of his definitive presentation of this field, his 1906 explanation of his work to his colleagues at the French Philosophical Society, and the article translated here, "La Science positive de la morale en Allemagne"—his first formulation of the program.

DURKHEIM'S ETHICAL THEORY

The development of the sociology of morals was only one of Durkheim's purposes in writing "La Science positive de la morale en Allemagne." His second purpose was to propose an ethical theory. Note the first paragraph of the essay: "In France we know only two kinds of ethics: that of the idealists and the Kantians on the one hand, and that of the Utilitarians on the other." The two aspects of Durkheim's thought were closely related. Durkheim's intent in proposing a sociology of morals as a distinct field within sociology was to develop a new basis for ethical theory.

Durkheim is not known today as a moral philosopher. Philosophers who now look at his ethical theory see immediately why it was unsuccessful. He thought, at least at the time of his earlier writings, that if one could analyze the moral structure of a society (the sociology of morals), then one could go on to improve that morality by eliminating its defects or abnormalities and by fostering its development to an even higher stage.

On the surface such a theory involves a blatant form of ethical naturalism in its move from the descriptive to the prescriptive. It presumes that one can draw judgments of what "ought

---

23. W. S. F. Pickering, ed., *Durkheim: Essays on Morals and Education,* 1979, London: Routledge & Kegan Paul, p. 92.

to be" directly from statements of what "is" without the aid of values or ethical principles which would require some sort of philosophical justification. Or, to put it another way, this type of theory presumes that one can determine what constitutes social progress (development to a higher social stage) without a philosophical justification of any criteria of what is to count as progress.

Philosophical and sociological rejection of this type of ethical naturalism constitutes the basis of the rift that has developed between sociology and ethics since Durkheim's time. Philosophers have devoted their attention to the question of how ethical or value principles might be justified so that one can speak about what society or social behavior ought to be, while sociologists have turned their attention to the "value free" analysis of social structures and social interaction. So clearly were the lines drawn between sociology and philosophy that neither sociologists nor philosophers ventured much further into the effort to describe the existing moral norms and beliefs of society. Avoided from both directions, the sociology of morals (which could have benefited as much from a philosophical clarification of its conceptual apparatus as from further sociological studies) went into a near total eclipse. Who now reads Wundt, Schmoller or Jhering, or, in Anglo-American circles, Spencer, Westermarck or Hobhouse?

Durkheim himself, as I shall show, gave up on sociological ethics of this naturalistic sort. His initial effort, however, was the most philosophically sophisticated of his age and is well worth noting despite its shortcomings.

Durkheim's perspective was contextual. Ethical thought, he believed, develops within the context of a society in which social norms and values, and even collective moral ideals, already exist. The justification of a moral claim (marital fidelity, for example) is situated in a society in which certain institutions (monogamy) already exist as norms and ideals. This contextual nature of ethical thought implies that ethical principles cannot be grounded in reason alone, intuition, a purely hypothetical social contract, or a utilitarian calculus. Durkheim did not entirely reject these forms of ethical argument, however; he was, in fact, alternatively interpreted as either a Kantian or a utilitarian. His point was that such reasoning presupposes the social structure and cultural context in which it is developed. Ethical theorists, Durkheim believed, generally choose some one aspect of society or human nature and develop it into a major principle. While this may be significant for the development of social values and moral ideals, the claims of each to universality or rationality cannot be justified.

Although this is not the place for an extended discussion of the contextual nature of ethical thought, it might just be mentioned that notions similar to Durkheim's point have reemerged in philosophical discussion in this century. John Rawls' position that his contractarian perspective is situated within a western liberal tradition limits the scope of his claims to a very general, but nonetheless particular, historical context. Alasdair MacIntyre and other communitarian theorists have contextualized ethics in a similar fashion. And J. L. Mackie's argument that ethics is necessarily relativistic (is his sense of the term) makes the same point.[24]

I have used the term "contextual" to express Durkheim's notion of ethical thought as grounded in a particular historical social and cultural reality because the normal connotations of the term "relativism" are too ambiguous. Relativism is generally taken to imply that ethical judgments *only* reflect the existing moral norms and values of a given society. Durkheim's relativism was primarily the social relativism of his sociological perspective. For Durkheim, to say that the *existing* moral norms and values of a society are relative is to state the obvious. "If there is one fact that history has irrefutably demonstrated," he said in his lectures on *Moral Education,* "it is that the morality of each people is directly related to the social structure of the people practicing it."[25] Not only are moral norms and values relative to the society in which they exist, according to Durkheim, the common or collective moral ideals of a society are relative in just the same way.

---

24. See John Rawls, *A Theory of Justice,* 1971, Cambridge, Mass.: Harvard University Press; Alasdair MacIntyre, *After Virtue,* 1981, Notre Dame, Ind.: University of Notre Dame Press; and J. L. Mackie, *Ethics: Inventing Right and Wrong,* 1977, London: Penguin Books.

25. Durkheim, *Moral Education,* p. 87; see *L'Education morale,* p. 74.

Individual morality, contrary what is often said, . . . is social even at its highest level. What it prescribes for us is the human ideal as society conceives it; but it is an ideal that each society conceives in its own image. The ideals of the Romans and the Athenians were closely tied to the particular organizations of each of these cities. The ideal type that each society requires its members to emulate is the keystone of its whole social system and gives it its unity.[26]

The consistency of Durkheim's social relativism had important consequences for his ethical theory in that it ruled out theories based upon the concept of a universal human nature. In his relatively unknown, but very interesting, lectures on *The Evolution of Educational Thought,* Durkheim criticized humanist doctrines which posit a unique and immutable human nature. "This assumption," he said,

constitutes the most flagrant contradiction of everything we know from the study of history. Far from being immutable, humanity is in fact involved in an interminable process of evolution, disintegration and reconstruction; far from being a unity, it is in fact infinite in its variety, with regard to both time and place. Nor do I mean simply that the external forms of life vary, that people do not everywhere speak the same language, wear the same clothes, or observe the same rituals. Rather it is the very basis of human mentality and morality which is perpetually in the process of transformation and is not the same here as it is there.[27]

What was true of human nature was also true, according to Durkheim, of rationality. "There are different systems of logic," he wrote, ". . . grounded equally in . . . the nature of society."[28]

The ethical implications of Durkheim's understanding of hu-

---

26. Emile Durkheim, *Sociologie et Philosophie,* 1974, Paris: PUF, p. 76; see Durkheim, *Sociology and Philosophy,* pp. 56–57.

27. Emile Durkheim, *The Evolution of Educational Thought,* 1977, London: Routledge and Kegan Paul, p. 324.

28. Ibid., p. 326.

man nature and rationality as socially and historically relative were quite apparent to him. "I see no justification," he concluded in a debate with Dominic Parodi, "for saying that the morality of one country or of one time is any more rational than the morality of another country or another time. Every morality has its own rationality."[29]

Durkheim's social relativism, however, did not lead him to an entirely naive ethical relativism. He did not hold that ethical judgments only reflect social norms or are justified only in relation to existing social values. He believed rather that it is possible to "improve" the morality of a society and that philosophers and other moralists can draw conclusions that go beyond the existing morality and guide social change. Exactly what constitutes "improvement" and how it can be determined is the crucial element of Durkheim's ethical theory.

Before considering Durkheim's ethical theory itself, I should note one other implication of his sociology of morals perspective. Since morality, according to Durkheim, is generated by human interaction, a diversity of norms, values and ideals develops not only between societies but within the same society. Since a society has different natural and associational groups with individuals filling appropriate roles, different sets of moral norms are generated. Morality differs according to sex ("the morals of a man are not those of a woman"[30]), according to age, social status, occupation, religious status and any number of other distinctions. While any ethical theory would certainly have to take account of the different duties and responsibilities associated with these different social roles, Durkheim thought that ethical theory might itself have to admit a plurality of perspectives. Why, he questioned, was it the objective of moral philosophy to reduce ethics to a single principle (utility, universality, etc.)? With reference to the sociology of morals he argued that the search for a single ethical principle that would subsume all of a culture's norms, values and ideals was contrary to the scientific method. With reference to ethics Durkheim chal-

---

29. Pickering, ed., *Durkheim*, p. 66.
30. Durkheim, *Professional Ethics*, p. 4.

lenged the notion that the ethical principles to which people are committed could, or even should, be reduced to a single principle.

Durkheim's Sociological Ethics

Durkheim's book *The Rules of Sociological Method,* published in 1895, could equally well have been entitled the "Rules of Ethical Method." While it contains Durkheim's well-known definition of sociological facts and an explanation of his methodology, a major portion of the work is devoted to a defense of his ethical theory. He stated this theory succinctly by drawing a comparison with medicine.

> For societies, as for individuals, health is good and desirable; sickness, on the other hand, is bad and must be avoided. If therefore we find an objective criterion, inherent in the facts themselves, to allow us to distinguish scientifically health from sickness in the various orders of social phenomena, science will be in a position to throw light on practical matters while remaining true to its own method. . . . The state known as health . . . is a valuable reference point to guide our actions. . . . It establishes the norm which must serve as a basis for all our practical reasoning.[31]

To lay the basis for his ethical theory, Durkheim devoted a chapter to the distinction between normal and pathological social behavior. Normal patterns of behavior for a society can be distinguished in two ways: first, Durkheim said, one looks to the average or statistically normal behavior, and secondly, one looks to the conditions of society. The latter mark is clearly, in Durkheim's mind, a functional or adaptational criterion. Both criteria are related, furthermore, to the evolutionary stage of the society in question. The functional criterion is necessary because when societies are in transition, behavior that is normal in a statistical sense may not reflect the pattern toward which the society is evolving. The ethical life, Durkheim said, "is a matter of working with regular perseverance

---

31. Emile Durkheim, *The Rules of Sociological Method,* S. Lukes, ed., 1982, New York: Macmillan, pp. 86–87.

to maintain the normal state, to reestablish it if it is disturbed, or to rediscover the conditions of normality if they happen to change."[32] It is the task of the politician, Durkheim added, to do for society what the physician does for the individual.

> The duty of the politician is no longer to propel society violently toward some ideal which seems attractive. His or her role is rather that of the physician: to forestall the outbreak of illness with good hygiene and, when it does break out, to seek to cure it.[33]

Naturalistic theories such as Durkheim's encounter a number of problems—most of which Durkheim eventually acknowledged. First, if the criterion of what is normal for a society is taken to be the average behavior, ethics would be reduced to mere conformism. The task of the sociological ethicist, as Durkheim put it, would be "to maintain the normal state." The statistical norm for the society would then become its ethical ideal and the good would be identical with the status quo. Durkheim knew, of course, that moral philosophers (he spoke of "moralists" in general) promote standards for the betterment of society which they advocate as "higher" than the existing standards, so the statistical norm could never serve as their only ethical standard.

Durkheim's second criterion of normality avoided the problem of accepting the status quo as ethically normative by employing a sociological determination of the "general conditions of collective life in the type of society under consideration."[34] Since the conditions of normality may change, according to Durkheim, the task of the sociological ethicist would be to "rediscover the conditions of normality" and assist society in adapting to them. The difficulty with this theory is that it presumes that the sociologist can, in the face of social change, project the new equilibrium toward which society is evolving. Durkheim's use of the phrase "type of

---

32. Emile Durkheim, *Les Règles de la méthode sociologique,* 1981, Paris: PUF, p. 74; see Durkheim, *Rules,* p. 104.

33. Durkheim, *Les Règles,* pp. 74–75; see Durkheim, *Rules,* p. 104.

34. Durkheim, *Rules,* p. 97.

society" is the key to this notion. Although he was not an uncritical follower of Comte or Saint-Simon in adopting a specific theory of social stages, he did believe that social types were, or would soon be, discernible and that sociologists would eventually be able to predict the course of social development. From the projection of this course of development, Durkheim thought, the evolution of moral norms could be determined. The sociological ethicist would then be able to tell, he said, "whether one particular mode of adaptation is better than another."[35]

Durkheim's second criterion of normality was no more successful than the first. Neither he nor any other sociologists have been able to project the course of development of a society with enough accuracy to determine a future state of equilibrium, much less develop a general theory of the evolution of social types.[36] In fact, the future development of any society would appear to be as much a product of the ethical values and ideals that a society chooses to adopt as vice versa. Curiously, Durkheim's sociology of morals allows for this in its emphasis on the evolution of social norms and ideals. His ethical theory, however, rested upon the possibility of social projections that his sociology of morals was unable to produce—unable not only in practice, but also theoretically since he understood the evolution of norms and ideals to be partially independent of other social factors. The requirements of his early ethical theory here are inconsistent with his multidimensional view of society.

Durkheim's Later Ethical Thought

After the publication of *The Division of Labor* and *The Rules of Sociological Method,* Durkheim's reliance on his naturalistic theory diminished sharply. His use of the normal/pathological distinction in his study of *Suicide* (1897) was quite limited. He said that a certain level of suicides was normal in society and

---

35. Durkheim, *Les Règles,* p. 50; see Durkheim, *Rules,* pp. 87–88.

36. In my *Emile Durkheim,* pp. 170–73, I have attempted to show that Durkheim was never able to apply this criterion successfully himself.

concluded that after the industrialization of Europe the level of suicides was abnormally high, but he offered no specific criterion for determining what that level was. While he made recommendations for the improvement of society, they were not dependent upon the normal/pathological distinction as an ethical criterion.

By the turn of the century Durkheim had given up on his naturalistic theory. In the *Rules* he had asserted definitively that "between science and art [i.e., the art of ethics] there is no longer any gulf; we may pass from the one to the other without any break in continuity."[37] In 1904, however, he agreed thoroughly with the position laid out by Lucien Lévy-Bruhl. Lévy-Bruhl, he said, "has no trouble showing that ethical theory does not constitute a science in the least degree."

> A science can reach conclusions which permit the establishment of norms, but it is not normative by itself. The notion of such a theoretical ethic is, therefore, a bastard; in it considerations which are properly scientific and theoretical are mixed with practical considerations, and in the end it is the latter which are preponderant, and by a good margin. . . . It is necessary, therefore, to renounce this contradictory conception of a normative science and to resolve to dissociate definitively science and practice.[38]

In 1909 Durkheim said only that sociological knowledge would permit us to determine the course of society "with greater reflection" than previously, and spoke of the process of drawing ethical judgments as involving conjecture "by analogy" with the past.[39]

A 1908 discussion with the philosopher Gustave Belot reported in the *Revue Bleu* confirms this change in Durkheim's thought in another way. In this debate Durkheim was critical of Belot's

---

37. Durkheim, *Les Règles*, p. 49; see Durkheim, *Rules*, p. 87.

38. Emile Durkheim, "Review of Lévy-Bruhl," *La Morale et la science des moeurs* (Paris: Alcan, 1903)," in *L'Année Sociologique*, VII, pp. 380–84, translated in Pickering, *Durkheim*, pp. 29–31.

39. "Sociologie et sciences sociales," in Durkheim, *La Science sociale*, pp. 142–43; See Traugott, *Emile Durkheim on Institutional Analysis*, p. 75.

claim to have developed a scientific ethic. In language that reflected previous criticisms of his own theory, he asked, "How does the objective study of moral facts permit new ends to be determined which are different from those that the given morality assigns to conduct?" and "How can the principle of a new moral orientation be created from even the complete systematization of moral data?" Durkheim then admitted that he himself was unable to make this crucial step between the sociology of morals and ethical theory. "I am raising the objection which has often been made to me," he said, "and I would be happy to see whether you are better able than I am to reply to it."[40]

Durkheim's failure to develop a comprehensive ethical perspective to replace his naturalistic theory did not, however, decrease his faith in the relevance of the sociology of morals to ethics. His starting point, he had said as early as 1888, was that one must study the existing morality of a society "attentively and respectfully before daring to modify it."[41] In 1903 he was equally convinced that only a sociology of morals "can furnish a rational basis for practical applications." Without appealing to any particular ethical theory, he still held that we must first understand the existing morality before attempting to intervene. Ethical intervention he felt is a matter of making changes that will help the system attain its own goals. "The more one becomes familiar with the laws of moral reality," he wrote, "the further along one will be in modifying it rationally, in saying what it ought to be."[42] At one point in his revue of Lévy-Bruhl's book, Durkheim posed the question of ethical theory rhetorically. "If theoretical morality is not a science of moral facts," he asked, "what is it?" His answer came close to renouncing ethical theory: "It is quite simply a way to coordinate as rationally as possible the ideas and feelings which

40. In Pickering, *Durkheim*, pp. 58, 57.

41. "Cours de science sociale: leçon d'ouverture," in Durkheim, *La Science sociale*, p. 107; See Traugott, *Emile Durkheim on Institutional Analysis*, p. 67.

42. Nandan, *Emile Durkheim: Contributions to* L'Année Sociologique, p. 130. "Revue de Lévy-Bruhl, *La Morale et la science des moeurs*," *L'Année sociologique*, 1904, VII, p. 384.

constitute the moral conscience of a definite period of time."[43]
Durkheim did, however, still appeal to the analogy with medicine,
not now to insist that the moral philosopher could emulate the
physician in applying scientific principles, but to point out that
physicians also practiced an art which they had to apply on a case-
by-case basis.

> Does it not happen constantly that the doctor becomes involved
> in problems for which physiology provides no solution? And
> what does he do then? He opts for the course of action which
> seems the most reasonable according to the present state of knowl-
> edge. Rational moral art will proceed likewise.[44]

Durkheim knew that this case by case method would not satisfy moral philosophers who "clamor for absolutes." "For them,"
he wrote, "the art of morality only appears true to itself if it decrees
precepts as though they are infallible." Durkheim's answer was that
the gaps between actual cases and the Kantian or Utilitarian theories
were just as disputable as the case by case judgment of Lévy-Bruhl's
method. "Seen in this light," he said, "all possible methods are
equally imperfect."[45]

In effect, Durkheim had given up on theoretical ethics for a
case by case or casuistic approach. In explanation of his ethical
perspective to the French Philosophical Society in 1906, Durkheim
said only that there were often clues in the facts themselves; sometimes, he said, society neglects its own moral principles and needs
to be reminded. At other times, he said, new norms or values are
developing which are so clearly related to other changes that they
can be recommended—this was clearly Durkheim's method in *The
Division of Labor*. The reverse of this, which Durkheim also mentioned, was that it could sometimes be judged that a certain moral

43. Nandan, *Emile Durkheim: Contributions to* L'Année Sociologique,
p. 128. See *L'Année Sociologique,* 1904, VII, pp. 382–83.

44. Emile Durkheim, "Review of Lévy-Bruhl, 'La Morale et la science
des moeurs' (Paris: Alcan, 1903)," in *L'Année Sociologique,* VII, pp. 383–
84, translated in Pickering, *Durkheim,* p. 32.

45. Pickering, *Durkheim,* pp. 32–33.

practice was out of date and needed to be discarded. "Historical research," he wrote, "can demonstrate that a certain moral practice is related to a belief which today is extinct and that the practice is thus entirely without foundation."[46] In the "Introduction to *La Morale*" which Durkheim left unfinished when he died, the same casuistic approach is apparent. Each realm or domain of morality needs to be studied, he said, to determine "the many precepts which constitute each part of morality, the causes that give rise to them, and the ends toward which they are directed." "Only then," he wrote, "is it possible to investigate how these precepts ought to be modified, rectified, or idealized."[47] Ethical theory appears to have become, for Durkheim, a matter of a casuistic approach to social change based upon projection and extrapolation from the sociology of morals.

"LA SCIENCE POSITIVE DE LA MORALE EN ALLEMAGNE"

My purpose here is to mention the major themes Durkheim developed in this article, to note the concepts and theories that became prominent in the later development of his sociology of morals, and to assess the influence of Wilhelm Wundt on his thought. First, however, a brief comment on the translation.

Durkheim often drew a careful distinction between philosophical ethics and the sociological study of morality. But since he believed at this time that an ethical theory could be derived from the study of morality, he had no problem using the term *morale* to signify either the sociological study of morality or ethics. As English usage has evolved, the terms 'moral' and 'morality' (except when used in phrases such as 'moral philosophy' or 'moral obligation') can easily refer to the established or existing moral norms of a society

---

46. Nandan, *Emile Durkheim: Contributions to* L'Année Sociologique, p. 145.

47. Durkheim, "Introduction à 'La Morale,' " *Revue Philosophique* (1920), Vol. 89, p. 94. See Pickering, ed., *Durkheim*, pp. 90–91.

as these might be studied sociologically. The terms 'ethics' and 'ethical,' on the other hand, generally imply a normative philosophical theory. Under "morality," the *American Heritage Dictionary* gives a definition of which Durkheim would surely have approved: "a set of customs of a given society, class, or social group which regulate the relationships and prescribe modes of behavior to enhance the group's survival."[48] Under "ethics," the same dictionary gives: "the study . . . of the specific moral choices to be made by the individual in his relationship with others; the philosophy of morals."[49] While I fully realize that 'morality' and 'ethics' are often used interchangeably, it serves my purpose here to have one term for the sociological study of morality and another for ethical theories, so I have adopted this usage.

In translating the text presented here it has often been easy to separate the sociological study of morality from ethical theory and to translate *la morale* as "morality" or "ethics" accordingly. But the sense of the term is not always so clear. When Durkheim had in mind the continuity he believed to obtain between the sociological study of morality and the development of an ethical theory, his use of *la morale* implied both. It is difficult to make an English expression imply both, no doubt in part because the continuity between the two lines of reasoning is not as direct as Durkheim then supposed. I have tried to use the phrase "moral theory" and the adjective "moral" where it seems to me that Durkheim had both in mind because the existing morality of a society can be understood to include the ethical theories held by its members.

The problem with the translation of the term *la morale* goes to the heart of the issue posed by this article, namely, the relationship between ethical theory and the sociology of morals. After considerable deliberation, I have decided to give this translation of Durkheim's article the title "Ethics and the Sociology of Morals" because it describes this double topic just as "La Science positive de la morale en Allemagne" described the topic in his day. I invite

---

48. *The American Heritage Dictionary of the English Language,* William Morris, ed., 1975, New York: American Heritage Publishing Company, p. 853.
    49. Ibid., p. 450.

the reader, however, to consider how the sense of certain passages in this essay would change if the term "ethics' were translated "morality" or vice versa.

Economists and Sociologists

The article, as I have said, is no mere account of current trends in German thought: it is, throughout, a critique by which Durkheim develops and presents his own views. This is what gives it special significance in the corpus of his writings. In Part I of the article Durkheim appealed to the German economists to criticize the Utilitarian analysis of society as the sum total of the interaction of individual interests. In effect, he used the German critique to establish his own social realism: society must be treated as an entity in its own right apart from the individuals who constitute it. Social facts are not just aggregates of individual facts; the interests and goals of society do not always coincide with those of its members— even the majority of its members. Morality, furthermore, is a product of society. Moral norms, values, and ideals are social creations— collective phenomena—not merely the products of individual consciousness. They have, moreover, a social purpose: to enable people to live together in ways that make society possible. The social realism described here became a central point of Durkheim's own social theory which he explained most forcefully in the doctrine of social facts elaborated in his *Rules of Sociological Method.*

The notion that moral norms develop naturally in the association of individuals can be traced in this article to Gustav Schmoller's theory that repeated actions become social habits which eventually turn into obligatory norms. Jean-Claude Filloux has shown just how central this idea is in Durkheim's thought. The "process of creative association," as Filloux calls it, generates moral norms interpersonally as products of group activity.[50]

---

50. Jean-Claude Filloux, *Durkheim et le socialisme,* 1977, Geneva: Droz, pp. 64–73. The later development of this concept can be found in Durkheim's *Moral Education,* pp. 60–62; *Sociology and Philosophy,* pp. 59, 91–92; and *Professional Ethics,* pp. 23–25.

An important implication of the social realism Durkheim found in the German economists was that economics could no longer be conceived as an autonomous realm apart from morality. Economic facts and moral facts (norms, etc.) are simply two types of social facts and must be analyzed together. The moral norms governing property, contracts or labor relations, Durkheim concluded, cannot be understood apart from the moral norms and values of a society any more than moral facts can be studied without reference to the economy. The article provides strong confirmation for what I have called Durkheim's multidimensional concept of society in contrast to commentators who read him as a thoroughgoing idealist.[51]

Finally, in the first part of the article Durkheim puts some distance between himself and the political program of the Academic Socialists. The social realism of the German economists had led some of them to believe that the economy could easily be controlled legislatively and that social planning could promote social (i.e., moral) goals. Durkheim was doubtful; he sided with Albert Schäffle's view that society was more like a natural organism and thus less amenable to state manipulation. This was a matter of degree, however, and did not negate Durkheim's interventionist ethical theory since the intervention he advocated stopped well short of comprehensive social planning.

Jurists

Part II of the article sets out some of the features of Durkheim functionalism. The German legal theorist Durkheim discussed here, Rudolf Jhering, departed from the prevailing legal positivism to construct a philosophy of law based on the function of law in society. "To explain a rule of law is not to prove that it is there," Durkheim here agreed with Jhering, "but to show that it is of use for something, that it is well adapted to the purpose it ought

---

51. Hall, *Emile Durkheim,* Chapter 11; see Jeffrey C. Alexander, *Theoretical Logic in Sociology,* 1982, Berkeley, Calif.: University of California Press, Vol. II, Chapters 4 and 8.

to fulfill." That purpose, he said, is characteristically related to the conditions of existence of a society.

Durkheim was critical of Jhering in a number of respects, however. First, Jhering seemed to him to hold that the purpose or goal of a social practice must be consciously intended by those who follow it. Durkheim's own view allowed not only for practices developing without any intended end which nonetheless later happened to meet a social need, but for unconscious motives as well. Stjepan Mestrovic's recent comments concerning the influence of Schopenhauer on Durkheim's understanding of human nature are supported by a number of passages in this article.[52]

Durkheim was also critical of Jhering's view that modern civilization, by comparison with ancient Rome at least, has restricted individual liberty. There are hints here of the notion Durkheim developed later in *The Division of Labor* that individual liberty can increase at the same time as social obligations become more complex. Finally, Durkheim noted that Jhering's approach to law demonstrated the necessity of a corresponding analysis of morality. The constraints of law cannot alone assure the existence of society. Jhering thus recognized the importance of morality, which by nature appeals to motives other than the fear of the law, for the maintenance of social order.

Wilhelm Wundt

The lengthy comments in Part III of the article on the *Ethics* of Wilhelm Wundt, which was just being published as Durkheim returned from Germany,[53] reveal a great deal about the later development of Durkheim's thought. Exactly how much of his analysis Durkheim owes to Wundt was a subject of debate even in his own day. In 1911 Simon Deploige, a Professor of Philosophy at the Catholic University of Louvain, published a book in which

---

52. See Stjepan G. Mestrovic, *Emile Durkheim and the Reformation of Sociology,* 1988, Totowa, N.J.: Rowman and Littlefield.

53. Wilhelm Wundt, *Ethics: An Investigation of the Facts and Laws of the Moral Life,* 3 vols., 1901–1908, New York: The Macmillan Co.

he argued that all of Durkheim's basic ideas were German. "At the end of this inquiry," Deploige asked with reference to the article translated here, "what 'French' elements remain?" "Certainly nothing weighty," he said (in case his readers had missed the point); "the German contribution is crushingly preponderant."[54] Deploige's own interest, however, was to discredit Durkheim in French circles for the purpose of advancing his own Thomistic position.

Durkheim did, in fact, develop a number of basic ideas on morality from Wundt's work. In his talk to the French Philosophical Society he specifically acknowledged Wundt's influence.[55] This influence, however, lay not so much in Durkheim's analysis of the role of morality in society as in the formulation and organization of the notion of a specific scientific study of morality. Wundt had, in effect, set out in his *Ethics* an outline of the sociology of morals Durkheim wanted to create. While the new German political economists and legal theorists had adopted a basic sociological orientation and had recognized the study of morality as an essential component of their task, it was Wundt who conceived morality as itself a field for scientific analysis. Wundt's formulation of the subject included definitions of the major concepts (norm, custom, motivation, etc.), a classification of moral facts, and a taxonomy of the various "departments" or domains of morality (family, civic, occupational, etc.). Wundt, furthermore, had attempted to bridge the gap between the scientific study of morality and ethics. In the third volume of his work he laid out a set of universal ethical principles.

In the comments above I attempted to show the significance of the sociology of morals program in Durkheim's thought. Even a brief outline of its contents is beyond the scope of this introduction.[56] It was developed, however, in Durkheim's lectures on *Moral Education* (which deal with many of the concepts found in Wundt's *Ethics*), and in his lectures on *Professional Ethics and*

---

54. Simon Deploige, *The Conflict between Ethics and Sociology,* Charles Miltner, tr., 1938, St. Louis, Mo.: B. Herder Book Co., p. 135.

55. Durkheim, *Sociology and Philosophy,* p. 49.

56. See Hall, *Emile Durkheim.*

Civic Morals (which take up Wundt's domains of morality). Durkheim's introductory lecture to his study of the family indicates that this work was also conceived as a part of the program. Taken together with his remarks to the French Philosophical Society and the unfinished manuscript of the introduction to his projected *La Morale,* one gets the strong impression that Durkheim intended to bring together his studies in the sociology of morals (none of these manuscripts were published in his lifetime) in a comprehensive work which, in its basic outline, would have paralleled Wundt's *Ethics.* The major influence of Wundt was thus in Durkheim's development of the research tradition which became the central programmatic orientation of his thought.

Rather than recounting Durkheim's presentation of Wundt, which is clear enough from the article itself, I want to note some of the major concepts Durkheim adopted from Wundt and then mention Durkheim's critique of Wundt's theory.

Social Facts

The development of social realism—the concept of society as an independent reality—was certainly one of Durkheim's major contributions to sociology. Durkheim himself attributed much of this perspective to the German theorists he studied. "Personally," he wrote in 1902, "I owe much to the Germans. It is in part from their school that I acquired the sense of social reality, of its organic complexity and development."[57] But Durkheim attributed as much or more of his concept of society to Comte. In reply to Deploige's specific charge that his social realism was a German notion, moreover, Durkheim said that he owed the basic axiom that the whole is not equal to the sum of its parts to the French neocritical philosopher Charles Bernard Renouvier (1815–1903).[58]

Whatever the origins of the general perspective of social realism

---

57. Quoted in Steven Lukes, *Emile Durkheim: His Life and Work,* 1973, New York: Penguin Books, p. 92.

58. Nandan, *Emile Durkheim: Contributions to* L'Année Sociologique, p. 160.

might be—or its status as an ontological or an epistemological asser-
tion, which Durkheim and his contemporaries appear not to have
distinguished clearly—the concept of social facts is much more specific.
A good deal of Durkheim's understanding of social facts, as set out
in the *Rules of Sociological Method,* can be traced directly to Wundt's
analysis of social customs by way of the article translated here.
"Collective phenomena," Wundt had said and Durkheim reported,

> do not come from individuals to be spread through society; they
> rather emanate from society and are then diffused among in-
> dividuals. Individuals receive them rather than create them.

Previous theorists had attempted to explain morality on the basis
of individual intuitions, motives and ideals. Wundt's social realist
perspective broke with this analysis, in large part through his
development of the field of social psychology as a distinct analytical
level of psychology. "There is only one way to understand collective
phenomena," Durkheim wrote, again paraphrasing Wundt, "that
is to study them in themselves."

Two characteristics of Wundt's analysis of social facts especially
captured Durkheim's attention. First, Wundt insisted that the origins
of social customs are to be found in other social phenomena, not
in individual states of consciousness and certainly not in hypotheses
concerning individual practices. Wundt traced the origins of most
social customs back to religious and juridical practices, which he
understood to be cooperative or intersubjective, rather than individual actions. Durkheim turned this point into a major rule of
his sociological method. When he later drew a sharp distinction
between causal and functional explanations, he insisted that social
origins ought to be sought for each.

> The determining cause of a social fact must be sought among
> antecedent social facts and not among the states of individual
> consciousness. . . . The function of a social fact must always be
> sought in the relationship that it bears to some social end.[59]

---

59. Durkheim, *Rules,* p. 134.

The second point of Wundt's analysis that attracted Durkheim's attention was the notion that social customs are distinct from individual habits in that they have an obligatory power which is external to the individual. Durkheim's formal definition emphasized this characteristic: "A social fact is any way of acting . . . which is capable of exerting an external constraint over the individual."[60]

In the "Preface to the Second Edition" of the *Rules*, Durkheim felt it necessary to explain that constraint was not the only characteristic of social facts, but just an external and immediate mark by which they could be recognized.[61] "La Science positive de la morale en Allemagne" makes it clear that from the outset Durkheim had in mind not only constraint, but the internalization of norms and the natural affinity individuals have for others as characteristic elements of social facts. The notion that Durkheim's "Preface to the Second Edition" indicates a radical change in his thought is not entirely correct.[62] While one can see a certain development in Durkheim's thought, the evidence here to the effect that constraint is "only an external sign and symptom of morality" and that other motives are involved, is enough to show that the development is not a reversal of an earlier position. Durkheim was not explaining away an inconsistency when he said in *The Elementary Forms of the Religious Life* in 1912 that he had "never considered [constraint] more than a material and apparent expression of an interior and profound fact."[63]

MORAL MOTIVES

The psychological counterpart of social constraint is fear of the consequences. If constraint is a characteristic of social facts, fear

---

60. Durkheim, *Les règles*, p. 14; see Durkheim, *Rules*, p. 59.

61. Durkheim, *Rules*, pp. 43–47.

62. See Lukes, *Emile Durkheim: His Life and Work*, pp. 13–14 and Jeffrey C. Alexander, *Theoretical Logic in Sociology*, 1982, Berkeley, Calif.: University of California Press, Vol. II, pp. 217–20.

63. Durkheim, *Elementary Forms*, p. 239n.

is one motive for conforming to the practice. While Wundt's definition of morality was a social definition, he was especially interested in the psychological dimension, the motivation of moral behavior. Durkheim recounts in some detail Wundt's threefold analysis of motives of perception, understanding and reason. Wundt's discussion of the goal or object of morality, furthermore, focuses upon the individual's interest in seeking the goal.

Durkheim incorporated a number of aspects of Wundt's analysis of moral motivation into his general definition of morality. In his most theoretical account of the nature of morality, his lectures on *Moral Education,* Durkheim adopted Wundt's view that the constraint of morality—or 'discipline,' as he called it there—could be traced to religious origins, what Wundt had called "the feeling of reverence for superhuman beings and powers."[64]

But there were, Wundt said, two fundamental psychological motives: the second being "the feelings of attraction to humanity." This second motive became the second "element" of Durkheim's definition of morality. Affection for one's fellow human beings, or what Durkheim described in the article translated here as "the affinity of like for like," became what he later called "desirability"[65] or the "attachment to society."[66]

Durkheim not only used Wundt's concept of attraction, he adopted Wundt's argument and repeated it in his later works. Actions that are entirely directed toward one's own self-interest, he said, are not what we commonly call moral actions. Morality is by nature other-regarding. But if one's own interest is an improper goal of moral action, then the specific interests of another individual cannot be a goal either. Therefore, the only actions which ought properly to be considered moral are those that are directed toward the welfare of society *as a whole.*

While this argument suited Durkheim's purpose of providing an essentially social definition of morality, it is inadequate in too many respects even to review here.[67] In substance, however, Durk-

---

64. Wundt, *Ethics,* Vol. I, p. 328.
65. Durkheim, *Sociology and Philosophy,* p. 45.
66. Durkheim, *Moral Education,* Chapters 4–6.
67. See Hall, *Emile Durkheim,* pp. 58–64.

heim's thought was based upon a social concept of human nature. "Human nature," he said, "is in large part a product of society."[68]

> There is in us a whole host of states which . . . society expresses in and through us. These states constitute society itself living and acting in us. . . . It is from society that we receive the most important part of ourselves. From this point of view one can easily see how society can become the object of our attachment.[69]

This "attachment," Durkheim explained, is an attachment to the whole of society including its ideals, so we are led to see actions that benefit society itself (apart from its individual members) as desirable. "We cannot perform an act," Durkheim concluded,

> which is not in some way meaningful to us simply because we have been commanded to do so. . . . Morality must, then, be not only obligatory but also desirable and desired. This desirability is the second characteristic of all moral acts.[70]

Durkheim also saw a direct correspondence between these two aspects of moral motivation and the ethical theories current in his day. This reinforced his notion that Utilitarianism and Kantianism had each emphasized only one side of the complex phenomenon of morality and that some sort of rapprochement between the two was necessary. Kant had emphasized the obligation or duty side of morality, but had utterly neglected people's attachment to society and their desire to do what they saw as good. For Kant, in fact, desire was an unacceptable moral motive. Utilitarianism, on the other hand, emphasized people's interest in doing what they saw as good, but neglected the inherent constraint of moral norms and the individual's sense of duty. In Durkheim's analysis, duty and the good are equally essential elements:

---

68. Durkheim, *Moral Education,* p. 69.

69. Durkheim, *L'Education morale,* p. 60; see Durkheim *Moral Education,* p. 71.

70. Durkheim, *Sociology and Philosophy,* pp. 44–45.

In fact, moral reality always presents simultaneously these two aspects which cannot be isolated. No act has ever been performed as a result of duty alone; it has always been necessary for it to appear in some respect as good. Inversely there is no act that is purely desirable, since all call for some effort.[71]

In his lectures on *Moral Education,* Durkheim added a third element of morality to his analysis which was drawn from Wundt's concept of the "Imperatives of Freedom." This element—the autonomy of the individual—was, according to Durkheim, a characteristically modern aspect of morality, that is, an historical development that had changed the nature of morality as a social fact. In "La Science positive de la morale en Allemagne," Durkheim said that Wundt's concept of an "Imperative of Freedom," being commanded to act autonomously, was something of a contradiction. Nevertheless, when he later set out his own analysis of the elements of morality, he included the third element, autonomy, along with the first two, discipline and attachment. The notion of autonomy in Durkheim's analysis is a complex and problematic matter which goes well beyond my purpose here. It will have to suffice to note that it refers, in large part, to the symbolic aspect of morality— ideals which individuals adopt for themselves.

DURKHEIM'S THEORY OF MORALITY

The concept of social facts and the analysis of moral motivation became key components of the theory of morality that Durkheim developed. A number of other elements of this theory are found in Durkheim's account of Wundt. First, there is the concept of society as the goal of morality. This is basically a functional concept: the function of morality, Durkheim said here, is to enable people to live together. Durkheim characteristically used the Aristotelian concept of the "end," "goal" or "object" (French *fin*) to express this notion.

---

71. Durkheim, *Sociology and Philosophy,* p. 45; see Durkheim, *Moral Education,* pp. 95–98 and Durkheim, *Rules,* p. 47, note 4.

The idea of morality as having the social function of enabling society to survive through facilitating solidarity appears over and over in Durkheim's writings. In his lectures on *Moral Education,* Durkheim demonstrated the social function of morality by distinguishing it from prudential and altruistic actions, as noted above. "Outside or beyond individuals," he said,

> there is nothing other than groups formed by the union of individuals, that is to say societies. Moral goals, then, are those the object of which is society. To act morally is to act in terms of the collective interest.[72]

Durkheim used a similar functional definition of morality as the basis of his discussion of the professional and civic realms. "There is no form of social activity," he said,

> that can do without the appropriate moral discipline. . . . There must be some organization that relates the social interests to the individual, that obliges him or her to respect them; and this organization can be nothing other than a moral discipline.[73]

In *The Division of Labor,* Durkheim's question was not so much whether morality had this social function, but whether a new moral regime—the division of labor—could fulfill this function adequately. The old (mechanical) morality, he said, "had as its function the prevention of all agitation of the common conscience, and, consequently, of social solidarity." The new organic morality, he concluded, has the same goal. The rule of specialization "has exactly the same function. It also is necessary for the cohesion of societies."[74]

A second point of Durkheim's theory of morality that is prefigured in Wundt's *Ethics* is what might now be termed the globalization of morality. Respect for religious commandments and the

---

72. Durkheim, *Moral Education,* p. 59.

73. Emile Durkheim, *Leçons de sociologie: physique des moeurs et du droit,* 1969, Paris: PUF, p. 53; see Durkheim, *Professional Ethics,* p. 14.

74. Durkheim, *The Division of Labor,* p. 397.

natural human affinity for others, according to Wundt, combine to turn egoism into altruism. Altruistic feelings attach first to those closest to us, the family, then to social classes, then to the nation, and finally to the ideal of a universal humanity. This theory of the evolution of a universal morality is found in Durkheim's *Moral Education*,[75] in the summary of his work he presented to the Philosophical Society,[76] in his lectures on socialism[77] and on *Professional Ethics and Civic Morals*.[78]

Finally, Durkheim also took over from Wundt the notion that different social groups generate their own sets of moral norms, values and ideals. The third volume of Wundt's Ethics provides an extended account of what he called the "Departments of the Moral Life." Durkheim's scheme included the family, professions and occupations, and citizenship as special social groups.[79] Durkheim's disciple and colleague, Marcel Mauss, recalled in 1925 that Durkheim's general account of social morality together with the morality of these special groups provided a comprehensive introduction to the field. "Durkheim had established," Mauss said, "the sociology of morals (*science des moeurs*)."[80]

Other concepts attributed to Wundt appear in Durkheim's later writings; Wundt contributed much to Durkheim's methodology for the study of religion, for example. But Durkheim also gave accounts of Wundt's ideas which he did not later adopt as his own; in particular, Wundt's extended analysis of ethical theories, which Durkheim later admitted as a possible subject for the sociology of morals but never undertook himself.

---

75. Durkheim, *Moral Education*, pp. 74–78.

76. Durkheim, *Sociology and Philosophy*, p. 52.

77. Emile Durkheim, *Socialism*, 1962, New York: Collier Books, pp. 170–81.

78. Emile Durkheim, *Professional Ethics*, pp. 70–74.

79. Ibid., Chapter 1.

80. Mauss, *Oeuvres*, Vol. 3, p. 480.

Durkheim's Critique of Wundt

The major point of difference between Durkheim and Wundt concerns Wundt's psychological perspective. While Wundt had agreed with the economists and sociologists of the new German school in emphasizing the social nature and function of morality, he had treated this as an unintended side-effect. The purpose of morality according to Wundt, Durkheim said, is really individual; it satisfies a psychological need for the individual to feel that he or she is not alone, but is part of an encompassing society. People seek, according to Wundt, an object greater and more permanent than their own existence to give meaning to their lives. Adopting moral norms, values and ideals makes the individual a part of a larger society. Wundt's account of morality was thus, in the end, a psychological or individualistic theory. He did not see society itself as the basic moral entity, nor was it an essentially social function that morality fulfilled.

Durkheim, by contrast, insisted upon the independent existence of society and, in fact, explained the individual as a product of society. His criticism of Wundt on this score was based on an appeal to the facts. If morality ultimately met an individual need, he argued, it would not seem coercive to the individual. But morality does, in fact, have coercive power. It is experienced as an external power that commands; society requires it of its members. Wundt's psychological account leaves this essential characteristic of morality unexplained. "What is desirable" (from the point of view of the individual), Durkheim wrote, "is not necessarily obligatory." In fact, Durkheim virtually reversed Wundt's account. What attracts individuals to society and gives them a sense of attachment, Durkheim said, is precisely the fact that morality is external—a product of society. It is not an individual need that makes morality effective for society, therefore, but the social need that makes morality effective for the individual. Durkheim's critique turned Wundt's psychological theory into a social theory.

A second point on which Durkheim differed from Wundt is related to the historical and comparative conclusions of Wundt's study and his ethical theory. Wundt found that the study of morality

led to the identification of a set of moral norms that were universal—
norms that were embodied in the diverse moral customs and theories
he analyzed. His project was, in fact, directed toward the isolation
and identification of these norms. Once such universal moral norms
were discovered, it was but a small step for Wundt to claim that
they constituted universal ethical principles. The universality of these
ethical principles, furthermore, was evidence of the common universal elements of human nature.

Durkheim objected to all this. There are, he said "as many
moralities as there are social types." The norms and customs studied
so far, he thought, had such diverse origins and functions that
the universal characteristics Wundt claimed to have discovered were
surely superficial. Nor is there any evidence, he concluded, of a
common universal human nature. "The old conception," he said
later, "according to which there is one natural morality and only
one, to wit, the morality that is based on the human constitution
in general, is now no longer tenable."[81]

Durkheim's critique of Wundt's universalism of norms, human
nature and ethical principles led him to a firm commitment to
moral and ethical relativism. Not only do societies have different
moral norms, he said later, but the morality of each is so closely
tied to its social structure that each morality can be said to be
ethically right for the society that generated it. "It is, indeed, impossible," he wrote in the *Division of Labor*, "to regard some practices as moral which would be subversive of the societies practicing
them. . . ."[82] Furthermore, since ethical principles are inherently
related to the societies which generate them, no ethical theory can
claim to be more rational in an absolute sense than any other.
"Every moral system has its own rationality," Durkheim said in
1909. "Roman morality has its rationale in Roman society just
as our morality has its rationale in the nature of contemporary
European society."[83]

---

81. Pickering, *Durkheim*, p. 31.

82. Durkheim, *The Division of Labor*, p. 423.

83. *Bulletin de la Société Française de Philosophie*, Vol. X, p. 60; see
Pickering, *Durkheim*, p. 65.

Durkheim's critique of Wundt was brief, but the points to which he took exception were major issues: Wundt's psychological orientation, which ultimately took morality to be a product of individual rather than social needs; Wundt's claim to have discovered universal characteristics of morality; and Wundt's ethical principles based upon the presumption of a universal human nature. For all that Durkheim adopted from Wundt in terms of his general approach to the sociology of morals, the differences on these issues make it difficult to view Durkheim as a follower of Wundt in a theoretical sense. It was in his programmatic orientation toward the sociology of morals and his demarcation of the field that Durkheim took up Wundt's project; but for Durkheim this was just the start.

Durkheim's Conclusions

The final Part of Durkheim's article, Part IV, is interesting. Durkheim devoted three quarters of it to his own analysis of the sociology of morals and only four pages to another German theorist, Albert Hermann Post. Durkheim noted the writings of Post not because they added much to the sociology of morals in a theoretical way, but because Post's attention to the details of the evolution of moral norms was an example of the kind of work he thought was necessary. Evolution here meant simply the study of historical development. Evolutionism, Durkheim said, should be understood not as a controlling model or theory, but simply as an historical approach to the problem—a "directive idea." Former theorists, and especially the British, had allowed it to dominate their investigations.

Durkheim added a final note on the social significance of his sociology of morals. The sociology of morals will not undermine people's confidence in their moral beliefs, he said, because it will show that these beliefs are the product of a long tradition and are essential to social solidarity. This is a more secure position, he believed, than that of the rationalist who may be led to abandon moral beliefs as soon as they are demonstrated to contain logical inconsistencies.[84]

---

84. See Durkheim, *Moral Education,* Chapter 1.

Durkheim devoted the major portion of the final part of the article to his own critique of ethics. The Kantians and the Utilitarians, he said, are both wrong: ethics cannot, at least at present, be reduced to a single principle, whether it is the satisfaction of human interests or rational duty. Each of these perspectives began with an important fact of moral experience, but made the mistake of elevating it into an exclusive principle.

In another respect, however, the Kantians and Utilitarians were both right: each had identified an essential aspect of morality. The perspective Durkheim proposed, which was the inductive method he discovered in the new German school of thought, must accept both aspects of morality. Ethics must be based on a sociology of morals that will take account of the whole reality of moral experience. Durkheim did not say how the Kantian and Utilitarian insights were to be combined, but he did propose a closer look at the existing morality before trying to improve it.

Durkheim's effort to reconcile Kant and the Utilitarians turned out to be a life-long project. One can follow it through his lectures and into the reviews of *L'Année Sociologique* and the debates of the first decade of the twentieth century. He never really resolved the problem. The merit of his ethical thought is his insistence that ethical theory has to come to grips with the actual nature and function of morality in the society in and for which ethical principles are developed. This means that the dual nature of morality must become an integral part of ethical thought—the actual obligations one finds imposed upon oneself by virtue of being a member of a society with specific socially defined roles, and the attraction of committing oneself to one's own and one's communal values and ideals. The ultimate outcome of Durkheim's sociology of morals perspective can be described as both "communitarian," inasmuch as it is embedded is a social context, and "casuistic," in that it approaches ethical problems on a case-by-case basis. The seeds of this perspective are contained in two paragraphs from the final part of the article which summarize his critique of the new German school:

The grave defect of all the works which we have analyzed so far is their extreme generality. Most of these moral theorists pose the same question as the spiritualists [Kantians] and Utilitarians, although it is true that they resolve it by a more scientific approach. They ask, straight off, what is the general formula of morality. Although they undertake to answer this question through an attentive observation of the facts, this manner of proceeding leaves morality in a situation which is quite exceptional among the other positive sciences. Neither physics, nor chemistry, nor physiology, nor psychology can be reduced to a single and unique problem; they consist rather of a multitude of particular problems which from day to day are becoming more specialized. No doubt the ultimate goal of the physiologist is to obtain knowledge of the nature of life while the goal of the psychologist is to obtain knowledge of the nature of consciousness; but the only way ever to obtain an adequate definition of either of these phenomena is to study in detail all of their particular forms, their nuances and varieties.

It is necessary to proceed in the same way with morality. The good, duty, and rights are not immediately given in experience. What we observe directly are particular goods, rights and duties. To discover a formula which will encompass them all, it is first necessary to study each one in itself and for itself, rather than to grasp, all in one breath, a general definition of morality. Is there not really something strange in posing these high questions when we do not know yet, or at best understand only very poorly, what property rights are, or contract, or crime, or punishment, etc., etc.? Perhaps the time for synthesis will come some day, but it hardly seems to have arrived yet. Therefore, the moral theorist can only respond by an admission of ignorance to the often repeated question, "What is, or better yet, what are, the ultimate principles of morality?"

BIBLIOGRAPHY

Works by Durkheim:

Bellah, Robert N., ed. *Emile Durkheim on Morality and Society.* 1973. Chicago: University of Chicago Press.

52   Ethics and the Sociology of Morals

Durkheim, Emile. *The Division of Labor in Society.* 1933. New York: The Free Press.
———. *The Elementary Forms of the Religious Life: A Study in Religious Sociology.* 1965. New York: The Free Press.
———. *Moral Education.* 1973. New York: The Free Press.
———. "La Philosophie dans les universités allemandes." 1887. *Revue Internationale de l'Enseignement,* Vol. XIII, pp. 313–38, 423–40.
———. *Professional Ethics and Civic Morals.* 1958. Glencoe, Ill.: The Free Press.
———. *The Rules of Sociological Method.* S. Lukes, ed. 1982. New York: Macmillan.
———. "La Science positive de la morale en Allemagne." 1887. *Revue philosphique,* Vol. XXIV, pp. 33–58, 113–42, 275–84.
———. *La Science sociale et l'action.* 1970. Paris: PUF.
———. *Sociology and Philosophy.* 1953. Glencoe, Ill.: The Free Press.
Nandan, Yash, ed. *Emile Durkheim: Contributions to* L'Année Sociologique. 1980. New York: The Free Press.
Pickering, W. F. S., ed. *Durkheim: Essays on Morals and Education.* 1979. London: Routledge & Kegan Paul.
Traugott, Mark, ed. *Emile Durkheim on Institutional Analysis.* 1978. Chicago: The University of Chicago Press.

Secondary Sources:

Bayet, Albert. *L'Idée de bien.* 1908. Paris: Alcan.
———. *La Morale laïque et ses adversaires.* 1925. Paris: Rieder.
———. *La Morale scientifique: essai sur les applications morales des sciences sociologiques.* 1907. Paris: Alcan.
———. *La Science des faits moreaux.* 1925. Paris: Alcan.
Belot, Gustave. *Études de morale positive.* 2 vols. 1921. Paris: Alcan.
Bouglé, Célestin. *The Evolution of Values.* 1926. New York: Holt.
———. *La Solidarisme.* 2nd. ed. 1924. Paris: Giard et Brière.
———. "Sur les rapports de la sociologie avec la morale." *Revue Pedagogique* 83:157–77.
Delvolve, Jean. *L'Organization de la conscience morale: esquisse d'un art morale positif.* 1906. Paris: Alcan.
Deploige, Simon. *The Conflict between Ethics and Sociology.* Charles Miltner, tr. 1938. St. Louis, Mo.: B. Herder Book Co.
Hall, Robert T. "Communitarian Ethics and the Sociology of Morals: Alasdair MacIntyre and Emile Durkheim." May 1991. *Sociological Focus* 24, no. 2.

Hall, Robert T. *Emile Durkheim: Ethics and the Sociology of Morals.* 1987. New York: Greenwood Press.

Karady, V. "La Morale et la science des moeurs chez Durkheim et ses compagnons." 1970. *Revue Universitaire de Science Morale* 12/13:85–114.

Lévy-Bruhl, Lucien. *Ethics and Moral Science.* 1905. London: Constable.

Mestrovic, Stjepan G. *Emile Durkheim and the Reformation of Sociology.* 1988. Totowa, N.J.: Rowman and Littlefield.

Parodi, Dominique. *La Conduite humaine et les valeurs idéales.* 1939. Paris: Alcan.

———. *Le Problème morale et la pensée contemporaine.* 1910. Paris: Alcan.

Ethics and the
Sociology of Morals

In France we know only two kinds of ethics: that of the idealists and the Kantians on the one hand, and that of the Utilitarians on the other. But there has recently emerged in Germany a school of moral theorists that has undertaken to develop ethics as a special science with its own methods and principles. The different branches of philosophy tend more and more to detach themselves from one another and to disengage themselves from the great metaphysical hypotheses which have bound them together. Psychology today is neither idealist nor materialist. Why should it not be the same with ethics?

The *Ethics* that Wilhelm Wundt published last October[1] has given a framework to these endeavors which until then had remained rather vague and poorly conceived both in themselves and in the goal toward which they were directed. To fully appreciate this important work, it is necessary to know the movement of which it is, one might say, the philosophical expression. This background is, moreover, all the more necessary since all these works are virtually unknown in our country. Nor are they only of historical interest. We shall see, in fact, that one can gather from them some valuable indications of the direction that ethics would take if one could elevate it to the ranks of science.[2]

---

1. Wilhelm Wundt, *Ethik: Eine Untersuchung der Thatsachen und Gesetze des sittlichen Lebens,* vi 577 pp. Stuttgart, 1886 [English translation, *Ethics,* 3 Vols. London, 1897].

2. Of course this is not the only movement in Germany at this time. The Kantians are still numerous and Utilitarianism has begun to assert itself; Herbert Spencer's *The Data of Ethics* has had more success than his other works. But there is nothing new in these two movements.

Part I

Economists and Sociologists

When Ribot[3] introduced German experimental psychology to the French public, he warned his readers that one would not find in Germany, as in England, just one or two schools of this character focussed around some great figures, but only a rather confused and impersonal discussion. Moreover, he noted that the progress of this psychology had been due not to philosophers, nor to professional psychologists, but to physiologists and to all sorts of other intellectuals.

Similarly, the ethical movement that we are discussing here has remained unknown and in part latent for a long time. It fills a need that a number of thinkers have felt simultaneously but which had not appeared in a determinate form. It gave rise to a number of views scattered throughout innumerable works, but which never came together and were not consolidated. In fact it is not with the ethicists, properly speaking, that these new ideas have emerged, but with the jurists and above all with the economists. It is from political economy that the whole movement started.

There has been, and still is, considerable discussion in France about "academic" socialism (*Katheder Socialismus*); but if the term is known, the reality is much less so.[4] The orthodox economists,

---

3. [Théodule-Armand Ribot (1839–1916), French psychologist, analyzed abnormalities of the memory in his *Diseases of Memory* (1881; Eng. trans., 1882).]

4. [Wagner, Schmoller, and Schäffle (discussed below) were prominent in the formation of the Union for Social Politics (*Verein für Sozialpolitik*) and were dubbed Socialists of the Chair or "academic socialists" (*Katheder Socialisten*) by the German press. The movement was basically state socialist,

who in our country retain the powerful influence that they have lost in the other countries of Europe, have done everything possible to misrepresent its spirit and character. They have seen in it only an excessive faith in power of the legislator and a superstitious respect for the authority of the state; they have not sought beneath these doctrines the profound cause from which they derive. In fact, what characterizes the new economic school is an intimate connection between political economy and morality that has revived both of these sciences at once.

Orthodox economists understand the relationship between ethics and political economy in three ways. For some the concept of ethics is reducible to that of utility; the two sciences are not distinct, the second includes the first. According to others, the two are independent but parallel; they develop side by side and share a mutual basis. This is the theory of those happy optimists who perceive in the social world nothing but perfect integration and providential harmony. All great moral truths correspond to economic truths, and all the more so if, from time to time, one admits a certain distant influence of ethics upon economics in matters of detail.

Finally, there is the more simple theory of those who deny the question. "Some have wanted to establish," says Maurice Block, "the connections that exist between political economy and ethics by finding among economic propositions, those that resemble certain

---

advocating that the government should both regulate business to prevent abuse and provide for some of the needs of the working class through social programs. Schmoller outlined the position as follows: "We preach neither the upsetting of science nor the overthrow of the existing social order, and we protest against all socialistic experiments. But we do not wish, out of respect for abstract principles, to allow the most crying abuses to become daily worse, and to permit the so-called freedom of contract to end in the actual exploitation of the laborer" (quoted in Harry W. Laidler, *History of Socialism,* New York, 1968). The academic socialists were especially influential on Bismarck, whose policy of social welfare programs in the 1880s simultaneously built worker loyalty to the state and undermined revolutionary workers' movements. Central to their theory was the view, shared by Durkheim, that the state has a moral responsibility for regulating the economy for the benefit of the community.]

moral propositions. . . . It seems to us that they are on the wrong track. The sciences are neither moral nor immoral; they state laws. Has anyone ever asked if mathematics or chemistry has any connection with ethics or religion?"[5] In other words, either they do not admit that there is such a thing as morality properly speaking, or they place it more or less outside of political economy.

The first of these solutions has never had many partisans in Germany which, until recently, has been unwilling to accept British utilitarianism. Ethics and political economy are rather conceived as distinct entities, but they carry on a constant dialogue with one another. It is this idea that radically distinguishes the German school from the British. "No doubt," writes Schoenberg,

> economic phenomena directly determine only the existence and the material situation of people. But the material condition, that is, the size and security of income, the extent of one's fortune, the nature of one's profession, etc., has a far reaching influence on people for it conditions their intellectual and moral state. In particular it exercises a decisive influence on the life of the family, on the support, the raising and the instruction of children, on the quality of the higher pleasures, on physical health and mental health, on behavior and on the attainment of all the moral objectives of life. These same phenomena also have a dominant influence on the strength and power of nations and on their role in the development of civilization. The capacity of a nation to defend its independence against foreigners and everything that it will be able to do for its intellectual and moral order, for the service of its ideals, for civilization, for art and for science essentially depend on the economic state of a society—on whether its wealth increases or diminishes.[6]

---

5. See his *Dictionnaire Politique* article "Sciences Sociales."
6. Schoenberg, ed., *Handbuch der politischen Ökonomie,* Part 1, p. 15.

Jean-Baptiste Say[7] or Bastiat[8] could, it is true, have signed this passage. But here is where the difference lies: for the orthodox economists, political economy produces its moral consequences quite naturally without need of any appreciable assistance or constraint. It is sufficient to let it alone.

For the German economists, however, this harmony of the two sciences and two modes of action which is so desirable is only a dream of the theorist, a hypothesis which the facts hardly confirm. Industrial progress and moral progress do not necessarily coincide. Consequently, since ethics is supposed to improve the world, it must exercise a regulative influence on political economy. The abyss that separates the two sciences is thus filled, but without mixing the two. The problem of political economy is ethical by nature; the goal it seeks is moral. "Social economy (*die Volkswirtschaft*) does not consist simply in corporate production. What is important above all is not knowing how to produce as much as possible, but to know how people live, to know the extent to which economic activity attains the ethical goals of life, the demands of justice, humanity, and morality which impose themselves upon every human society."[9]

Nevertheless, we must recognize that these formulas, with which economists are so often content, lack precision. One should see them less as scientific doctrines, properly speaking, than as noble aspirations along with a confused apprehension of poorly analyzed facts. The two sciences are connected, but one cannot see their relationship; they touch without penetrating. It even seems that one could treat each of them apart from the other, leaving for later the question of their relations and of tempering the economic

7. [Jean-Baptiste Say (1767-1832), Professor of Industrial Economics at the Conservatoire des Arts et Métiers and of Political Economy at the Collège de France, was noted for his law of the free market which postulated that supply creates demand and for his distinction between the entrepreneur and the capitalist.]

8. [Frédéric Bastiat (1801–50), French economist and proponent of the free trade economics of Adam Smith, founded the Association for Free Trade in 1846 and edited its journal *Le Libre-Échange.*]

9. Schoenberg, ed., loc. cit. See also pp. 54ff.

laws to put them into agreement with the maxims of morality. The new economic school, says Menger, does not replace the old, but is content just to bring ethical judgment to bear upon the truths the old school had established;[10] and this criticism is equally true of some of the academic socialists. To make the complete intimacy of political economy and ethics clear, it is not enough to show by a few examples that economic activities have moral implications. Since everything in the world is related, there is nothing astonishing in the fact that two parts of the same reality react with one another. It is rather necessary to prove that these two orders of facts, while being entirely distinct, are really of the same nature. It is this demonstration that Wagner and Schmoller have undertaken, the former in his handbook of political economy,[11] the latter in his paper entitled "On Some Fundamental Questions of Law and Social economy."[12]

---

10. Karl Menger, *Untersuchungen über die Methode der Socialwissenschaften,* Leipzig, 1883, Chap. VI, VII, and Appendix IX. [Carl Menger (1840-1921), Professor at the University of Vienna, was a founder of the Austrian school of economics. His *Principles of Economics,* translated into English in 1950, is now recognized as a classic in the history of economics. Menger developed marginal utility models which set the standard for modern microeconomic analysis. It was his interest in the history of social institutions and the history of economic theory, however, that attracted Durkheim's attention.]

11. Adolf Wagner, *Lehrbuch der politischen Ökonomie,* Leipzig, 1879, Vol. I, esp. part 2 (pp. 343-821). [Adolf Wagner (1835-1917) Professor of Political Economy at the University of Berlin for forty-six years, was a philosopher of conservative state socialism. The proper role of the state, he thought, was not only to regulate economic activities, but to undertake redistributive social programs designed to build social solidarity. He envisioned an alliance of civil servants, traditional landholders and the working class which would act as a counterbalance to the growing power of the industrial and commercial elites. His later thought became extremely nationalistic and anti-Semitic.]

12. Gustav Schmoller, *Über einige Grundfragen des Rechts und de Volkswirtschaft,* Jena, 1875, see esp. chapter III entitled "Wirtschaft, Sitte, und Recht" (Political Economy, Mores, and Law). [Gustav Schmoller (1838-1917) was Professor of Political Science (which included economics and public administration) at the Universities of Tübingen, Halle, Strasburg and Berlin. Coming from the civil servant class, he was aligned with the monarchy but

For the Manchester School, political economy consists of the satisfaction of the needs of the individual, especially his or her material needs. In this conception the individual is the unique goal of economic relations; it is both by and for the individual that everything is done. Society, on the other hand, is an abstraction, a metaphysical entity, which the scientist can and should ignore. What one refers to by this term is only the interrelationships of individual actions; it is a whole which is nothing more than the sum of its parts. In other words, the great laws of economics would have been exactly the same even if there had never been nations or states in the world; these laws presuppose only the presence of individuals who exchange their products. At base, the liberal economists are the unwitting disciples of Rousseau whom they wrongly disavow. They acknowledge, it is true, that the state of isolation is not ideal; but like Rousseau they see in social bonds only a superficial relationship determined by mutual interests. They conceive of the nation only as an immense corporation through the actions of which each person receives only as much as he or she gives, and where one remains only if one is justly rewarded. Moreover, it seems to them good that it is this way; for a collective life that is too intense would quickly become a threat to the independence of the individual which is more precious to them than anything. So the more consistent of these theorists do not hesitate to declare that national sentiments are only the remains of prejudice bound to disappear some day.[13] Under these condi-

advocated strong government regulation of working conditions. Schmoller was a leading member of the Academic Socialists (*Verein für Sozialpolitik*) but opposed the democratic wing of the movement because he felt that an expansion of democratic rights would lead to bourgeois domination and further class struggle. A dominant figure in both government and academic circles for over thirty years, Schmoller's inability to separate his scientific theories from his political advocacy provided the background for Max Weber's arguments for eliminating value judgments from the social sciences.]

13. See G. Molinari, *L'Évolution politique,* Paris, 1884. [Gustave Molinari (1819–1912), political economist and editor of *Journal des Économistes* and *Journal des débats,* argued that the free market would establish a natural equilibrium in labor and exchange.]

tions economic activity can have no other motive than self-interest. Political economy is thus radically separated from morality, if indeed any ethical ideal is left for humanity once all social bonds are dissolved.

It is this concept that Wagner and Schmoller attack. For them, on the contrary, society is a real being which certainly does not exist outside of the individuals who compose it, but which nonetheless has its own nature and personality. Current expressions such as "social conscience," "collective spirit," "the body of the nation," do not have simply a linguistic value; they express facts which are eminently concrete. It is false to say that the whole is equal to the sum of its parts. For from the fact that these parts have definite relationships and are assembled in a certain way, there results something new: assuredly a composite entity, but one with special properties which can under certain conditions even be conscious of itself. Society is not, therefore, reducible to a blurred mass of citizens. Since the social being has needs which are its own, some of which are material, it institutes and organizes for their satisfaction an economic activity which is not that of one individual or another nor of the majority of citizens, but of the nation in its entirety. This is what is meant by the term *Volkswirtschaft* (social economy) of which our economists have seldom understood the sense, but which sums up and characterizes this whole economic philosophy. "The *Volkswirtschaft*," says Wagner," is like the term people: a real whole. Private economies (*die Einzelwirtschaften*) are, not parts, but members of it."[14] Far from being a logical abstraction, social economy—if, for lack of a better term, this is how we can translate *Volkswirtschaft*—is the true concrete reality, and it is private economy which becomes an abstraction if one tries to make it totally independent rather than seeing it as part of a whole. Private economy has a place in science only as an element of the collective economy, which becomes in this way the immediate subject of political economics. In other words the science of economics is concerned first with social interests, and only as a consequence with the interests of individuals.

---

14. *Handbuch,* p. 68.

then imposes itself on our will with the force of an obligation. We feel ourselves compelled to cast all our actions in this same mold. It is the same with social relations as with incidents of our private behavior. After an initial period of groping about and instability they become fixed, taking the form that one recognizes from experience to be the best, and henceforth we are ourselves bound to conform to them. This force of obligation is, moreover, not only the authority of common usage; it is a feeling, more or less clear, that it is required by the public interest. This is how mores are formed which are the first seeds from which law and morality are subsequently born; for morality and law are only collective habits, constant patterns of action which come to be common to a whole society. In other words, it is like a crystallization of human behavior; and economic phenomena, just like others, are susceptible to crystallization. No doubt they must not be locked into forms that are too rigid. As the milieu in which we move becomes daily more complex and more flexible, we must have enough initiative and spontaneity to follow it in all its variations, to change with it as it changes. But on the other hand it must not be thought that chaos and incoherence reign supreme in the economic world. Once they have cut their course, the phenomena that flow there do not change capriciously. With time the economic life develops a course to which the matter that flows through it must yield. Economic patterns thus become moral phenomena.

If the orthodox economists and moralists of the Kantian school place political economy outside of morality, it is because these two sciences seem to them to study two worlds with no connection between them. But if there is no other difference between the two than that between the container and the contents, then it is impossible to abstract the one from the other. One understands nothing of the maxims of morality regarding property, contracts, labor, etc., if one does not understand the economic causes from which they are derived. On the other hand, one would have a very false idea of economic development, if one were to ignore the moral causes that intervene in that development. Ethics is not absorbed by political economy. Rather, all social functions contribute to the production of the form to which economic phenomena have to be subjugated while they contribute to its production.

For example, to the extent that society needs increased production it is necessary to stimulate greater personal initiative, and consequently, law and morality allow each person a much greater share of personal liberty. But at the same time, and under the influence of causes which are only slightly related to economic necessities, the recognition of human dignity emerges and opposes the abusive or premature exploitation of women and children. These protective measures dictated by ethics react in turn with economic relations and transform them by motivating the industrialist to replace human labor with that of machines.

"Political economy and the philosophy of law," says Wagner,

> ought to be considered sciences that are complementary to one another. We especially need the philosophy of law in questions of the fundamental necessity of the state for social life, of its scope, . . . of the manner in which laws concerning ownership, contract, and succession are organized by the state, of the implementation of the principle of distributive justice in the apportionment of social goods and services and communal obligations. But just as political economy needs to be in contact with the philosophy of law, so the philosophy of law, to the same degree and for its own interests, needs to feel itself in contact with the actual law of the social economy.[15]

But since until now this method has hardly been practiced by philosophers, the economist must formulate his or her own philosophy of law, and this is in fact what Wagner has undertaken in the second and more important part of his work (*Recht und Verkehrsrecht*).

Applying this method to personal rights he shows that, regardless of what has been said about it, individual liberty has no absolute value in itself. It has, on the contrary, some serious disadvantages that must be averted by limiting it. Currently, in

---

15. Adolf Wagner, *Lehrbuch der politischen Ökonomie,* Leipzig, 1879, Vol. I, p. 290.

our societies liberty is only ethically acceptable if it is restrained. Moreover, the author is not satisfied with vague generalities on the abstract concept of liberty, but analyzes in detail the concrete forms it takes in practical life: freedom of movement, of travel, of immigration and emigration, of marriage, etc. He observes the multiple consequences that each of these rights entails, weighs the advantages and disadvantages, and marks the limits. He proceeds in the same manner for property rights. He does not seek to establish or deny the right of ownership in the abstract, but distinguishes the ownership of personal property from real property and then within the latter, agricultural and urban property, the ownership of mines, forests, roads, etc. He submits each of these to special examination and arrives at a conclusion which is quite complex, to be sure, but which keeps close to the facts and can for this reason have practical applications. "Ownership," he says, "is the highest form of juridical power recognized in law which a person can exercise over things." There are thus limits which vary with time and place and different sorts of property, but which, at each point in history, are determined by law and not by the sovereign will of the individual.

We shall not consider the details of these analyses; what should interest us above all in this movement is not this or that particular idea to which it has given birth, but the direction it imparts to the study of morality. Until now, for every school of ethics, for the Utilitarians as much as for the Kantians, the problem consisted essentially in determining the general forms of ethical behavior from which one would later deduce the substance. One began by establishing that the principle of ethics is the good, or duty, or utility and then from this axiom one drew a few maxims that constituted practical or applied ethics.

The works we have just reviewed, however, show that here, as elsewhere, form does not precede substance, but derives from it and expresses it. One cannot construct an ethic in its entirety and impose it on reality later; one must rather observe reality to infer morality from it. One must grasp ethics in its many relations with the innumerable facts on which it is patterned and which it regulates in turn. If one detaches it from them, it seems not to be related to anything but to float in a void. Apart from any interrelationship with the source of life itself, ethics withers away to the point of being reduced to nothing more than an abstract concept, contained entirely in a dry and empty formula. On the other hand, if one leaves it in relationship with the reality of which it is a part, it appears as a living and complex function of the social organism.

Nothing of any importance in society can happen which does not incur a reaction from morality and retain its mark. The economists, it is true, have only attracted our attention to certain of these facts which particularly interest them; but it is easy to generalize the conclusions at which they have arrived. If they are right, we can no more separate morality radically from political economy, statistics, or the positive science of law, than we can study the nervous system in abstraction from other organs and other functions.

But if morality is bound to societies to such a degree, it must have a part in their destinies and change at the same time that they change. The philosophy that has until recently reigned in Germany, however, held that it was possible to deduce from human nature in general an immutable ethic valid for all times and places. This is what is still known as the philosophy of natural law (*Natur-recht*). One of the great services that the German economists have rendered was precisely to contest this doctrine and to show, with the help of history, that among our laws and moral obligations there is none that has not been unknown at sometime or other, and rightly so. The philosophers try to establish by formal arguments that human beings are made for absolute freedom; but the historian teaches us not only that slavery was a universal fact in antiquity, but even that it was useful and necessary. If the chief of a horde or a barbarian tribe took a notion one day to give to his subjects the independence we enjoy today, this would have done away with all collective life. When one places ethics outside of time and space, one can no longer return to the facts. If these supposed eternal verities had ever applied to particular societies, they would have brought about their dissolution. So whatever the origin or the final object of ethics might be, it is certain that it is a science of life;

above all it has the function of enabling people to live together. If, then, it becomes a source of death, it ceases to be itself and changes into its opposite. Therefore, the fundamental vice of every such doctrine is that it rests on an abstraction. This notion of a general humanity, always and everywhere the same, is only a logical concept without objective value. Actual humanity, humanity that is truly human, evolves like the milieu that encompasses it. Furthermore, what changes easily in us are our inclinations, the dispositions which make us social beings. Just because they are so complex, they can and must be susceptible to change more quickly. Since it is in this part of our nature that law and morality have their roots, it is not surprising that they are transformed more quickly than our logical reasoning or our aesthetic faculties.

If the academic socialists acknowledge the evolution of ethical ideas, it is because they need this point to establish the theses that they hold dear. In fact, what brought about the schism between the orthodox economists and the others historically was not the entirely speculative question of the relationship between political economy and ethics. A problem of practical interest started the rift. It was the question of whether the organization of the economy could be transformed by human intervention. For the Manchester School the laws of economics are no less natural then the laws of gravity or electricity and are therefore immutable: one can manipulate them and use them, but not modify or suppress them. The German mind could never accept this economic fatalism. On the one hand, it seemed to them that it would be giving up too quickly to declare such desirable changes impossible. On the other hand, they had demonstrated historically that these presumed natural laws had changed remarkably with time. But then it became necessary to discover among the phenomena of economics those elements that would be flexible enough to permit these changes. If economic phenomena really only lend themselves to the influence of material causes like the number of inhabitants and the levels of supply and demand, etc., this would scarcely leave room for contingencies. But it is not the same if economic phenomena also contain moral elements because these, since they are more flexible, lend themselves more easily to transformation.

If the economists had affirmed nothing more, their doctrine would be unobjectionable. Unfortunately, they have been carried away by their practical preoccupations, and have drawn some conclusions from these truths which are not a bit scientific. From the fact that moral phenomena are more changeable than others, they have concluded that they can be transformed by legislators at will. Because moral phenomena have their origin not in the nature of material objects, but in the human consciousness, the German economists have seen them as artificial constructions that the human will can destroy or rebuild since it created them in the first place. "Social economy," says Wagner,

> is an organism, but it is not for that reason a natural product. From a certain point of view it is surely a natural product like the nation itself. Like the nation in a certain way it owes its existence, its duration and its development to natural human tendencies such as the instinct for self-preservation and the sexual instinct. . . . But at the same time it is the creation of conscious human activity, an artificial product (*ein Gebilde bewusster menschlichter That, ein Kunstproduct*). It is the human will directed toward a definite end and acting according to a preconceived plan that has given the social economy its intentionally determined form.[16]

But for contemporary psychology, psychological, moral and social facts, however elevated and complex they might be, are nevertheless natural phenomena in the same category as any others. The social realm, i.e., moral laws, is only distinct from other natural realms by nuances and differences in degree. No doubt change is easier in the social realm since the substance is more elastic, but change is not produced magically by order of the legislator; it can only come about through interaction with natural laws. In any case, it is nearly always impossible for social change to be created with methodical reflection. This is again a psychological truth that our economists seem to ignore. Most social facts are much too complex

---

16. Adolf Wagner, *Lehrbuch der politischen Ökonomie*, Leipzig, 1879, Vol. I, pp. 201–202.

to be able to be embraced in their entirety by human intelligence, however vast it might be. The majority of moral and social institutions therefore, are due not to reason or calculation but to obscure causes, to subconscious feeling, and to motives which have no relationship to the effects they produce and which, consequently, they cannot explain. Finally, the academic socialists do not perceive that they are reviving Rousseau (whom they attack), and are upholding one of his most cherished theories; for they also finally came to see the higher functions of society as only artificial arrangements without any connection to the nature of things. This is where their excessive confidence in legislative action comes from: this predilection for authoritarian means for which they are so often reproached and which discredits their doctrines among a great many good minds.

Schäffle[17] is the first one to have separated out the ethical implications of this economic movement, ridding them, at least in great part, of the serious error that we have just noted. This is not to say that Schäffle is an academic socialist; he separates himself as much from Wagner as from Karl Marx, and is—contrary to what has been said in France—neither a collectivist nor a state socialist. He is not a member of any school; his doctrine has its own features which keep it distinct from any other. It is beyond question, however, that the new economic school in Germany has had a profound effect on the development of his thought and it is permissible to associate him with it, provided that one distinguishes him from them carefully.[18]

---

17. [Albert Eberhard Frederich Schäffle, Professor of Economics at the Universities of Tübingen and Vienna, Austrian Minister of Trade and journalist, was known for his analysis of society as an organic system. Like the academic socialists, he was strongly opposed to the liberal economics of the Manchester school, but felt that government intervention in the economy should be based upon an analysis of the natural development of the system rather than upon economic theory alone. His most popular work, *The Quintessence of Socialism* (1875) was translated into English in 1889.]

18. Moreover, Schäffle admits the ethical character of political economy as do the academic socialists. See in his *Gesammelte Aufsätze*, Tübingen, 1885, the two studies entitled *Mensch und Gut in der Volkswirtschaft* (*Hu-*

In his *Bau und Leben des socialen Körpers* Schäffle sets out
the general principles of ethics.[19] The author especially applies himself to defining law and morality and to showing how they differ
and complement one another. Actually, the definition he gives is
a little lacking in clarity and precision. According to him, an action
is only moral if it is the result of an internal impulse. It is a spontaneous movement of the conscience, a burst of free will (*die Selbst-
bestimmung des Willens von innen heraus*) which the slightest
external pressure would immediately cause to lose its character.
Law, on the contrary, consists in an external act determined by
an equally external will. Morality among living beings corresponds
to the spontaneous energy with which every cell, tissue, and organ
discharges its own function and collaborates toward the collective
health of the organism. The law corresponds rather to the actions
and reactions of different organic units on one another, to the
movements which adjust them and assure their harmony. But is
this not a unique restriction on morality to make it consist solely
of the free dispositions of the will? It is certainly questionable,
furthermore, whether the commands of morality are exempt from
all constraint; the constraint here is only less overt and less violent.

One should not, however, attach too much importance to these
definitions; they can only be general and approximate since the
author does not propose to construct an ethical theory. What is
more important is that Schäffle clearly recognized the empirical
and organic character of morality and law. Morality is not a system
of abstract rules that people find inscribed in their consciences or
that the moral philosopher deduces in the privacy of his or her
office. It is a social function or, even more, a system of functions
which is formed and consolidated under the pressure of collective
needs. Love in general, the abstract tendency toward unselfishness,
does not exist. What actually exists is love in marriage and in

---

manity and the Good in the Social Economy) and *Die ethische Seite der
national-ökonomischen Lehre vom Werthe* (*The Ethical Dimension of the
Economic Theory of Value*).

19. Vol. I, 550–674; Vol. II, 59–81, Tübingen, 1875. On the particular
forms of law, *passim*.

the family, the free devotion of friendship, civic pride, patriotism, the love of humanity; and all these feelings are products of history. These are the facts that constitute the substance of morality. The moral philosopher can, then, neither invent them nor construct them; he or she must observe them wherever they exist and then seek their causes and conditions in society. No doubt the sense of the ideal, this need that pushes people to be discontent with anything relative and to seek an absolute which they cannot attain, intervenes in the evolution of moral ideas; but it does not create them. On the contrary it presupposes them and can only give them a new form.

But while Schäffle like the academic economists intends to treat morality and law as organic social functions, he does not posit the excessive flexibility that Wagner attributes to them. The laws of morality are natural laws derived from human nature and the nature of society; they are products of an evolution that is unique to human societies the course of which one cannot change arbitrarily. For Wagner and Schmoller society is, at least in part, a machine that one can change from the outside; with Schäffle it really becomes a living being that changes from within. The legislator does not invent its laws; he or she can only ascertain them and formulate them clearly.[20] They develop from day to day progressively in our everyday relations inasmuch as we sense a need for them; they express the conditions of our mutual adaptation. But these conditions can neither be foreseen nor calculated *a priori*. One can only observe and establish them with as much precision as possible when they are in balance. They are, then, the communal work of a society; legislators do not play the extensive role in their formation that the academic socialists have assigned to them, and the importance of legislators diminishes in proportion as that of society grows.

Schäffle also speaks of the dangers of legislative influence and

---

20. "Die Positivirung des Rechts ist also kein Schaffen sondern ein Finden." ("The enactment of laws is therefore not a creation but a discovery.") See, on this subject, Fricker, "Das Problem des Völkerrechts," *Zeitschrift für die gesamte Staatswissenschaft,* 1872, 92.

of the advantages of individual initiative in terms that a disciple of Bastiat could employ. So when one sees certain economists reproach him for having a tendency toward authoritarianism, one tends to fear that they have only read his books superficially. Schäffle certainly believes, contrary to the orthodox economists and to certain moral philosophers, that moral and economic laws are subject, in the course of history, not only to slight changes but to profound transformations. But he concludes that these transformations result from internal causes and not from exterior and mechanical pressures.

It would be an exaggeration, however, to say that Schäffle sees only differences of degree between the facts of the moral life and the other phenomena of nature; his evolutionism is much more moderate. According to him, what radically distinguishes moral and social phenomena from all others is that they are self-conscious and deliberate. Schäffle is thus led to allowing reflection to play an excessive role in the formation of human societies and in the genesis of moral ideas. What creates all great moral institutions, says our author, is the awareness of the ends they must serve. This conscious representation of goals is characteristic of social organization in general.

It is rather difficult, however, to reconcile this theory with the previous one, since reflection produces works of art, not of nature. Reflection is embodied in artificial machines that we build, not in living organisms. If social goals could be grasped with such assurance, they could be projected, submitted to calculation and to logical configuration. Then individual initiative would cease to be so necessary. Nothing is more flexible than ideas; they react to minor changes without difficulty and sometimes evolve with extreme rapidity. If society is an organism built upon clear ideas, it is endowed with a tremendous malleability which is bound to tempt the legislator into action.

There is an express contradiction here which is undeniable. Schäffle repeatedly calls society a product of art (*ein Produkt der Kunst*), but he only recognizes one social group as truly natural, the family, because it owes its origin to a physiological fact. It is probable that this contradiction is caused by the present state of German psychology. In fact, German psychologists make the psychic life out to be something entirely distinct in the world. They all say more or less explicitly that there is a break in the continuous scale of being; for them the word *Natur* designates nature exclusive of humanity.[21] The realm of humanity comes under absolutely special laws. This is no doubt the origin of the intellectualism that German moral philosophy and sociology are having some difficulty shaking.

In conclusion, the results of this movement can be formulated thus: for a number of years we have witnessed a genuine dismemberment of the old philosophy. Already psychology has gained its independence; what has extracted it from the realm of the philosophical sciences is the affinity it has with the biological sciences. No doubt the day will come when it will be completely autonomous. In the meantime, however, it has profited infinitely from being in contact with physiology. The study of morality in Germany is in the process of passing through the same crisis; more and more it ceases to revolve around metaphysics and general philosophy, drawn as it is into the sphere of influence of the social sciences. It is through these that it will emancipate itself. This is why economists have been the initiators of this transformation.[22]

---

21. See our article on "La philosophie dans les universités allemandes," *Revue Internationale de l'Enseignement,* 13 (1887), pp. 313–38, 423–40.

22. One might be perhaps surprised to see that we have said nothing of Lilienfeld who, in various passages of his *Gedanken ber die Socialwissenschaft der Zukunft,* Mitau, 1873, has expressed ideas quite close to those that we have just described (see especially Vol. I, ch. 27 and Vol. III, ch. 11). The reason is that Lilienfeld does not belong to the movement we have been studying. All the moral theorists mentioned here see in moral phenomena *sui generis* facts which must be studied in themselves, for themselves, and by a special method. On the contrary, Lilienfeld's unique objective is to show the analogies between societies and organisms. While the conclusions sometimes coincide, the object and the spirit are totally opposite.

Part II

The Jurists

Rudolf Jhering

If morality is a function of society, then it is related not only to economic facts but to all the social facts from which it is derived and which form its content. The part of ethics called the philosophy of law ought then to find its material in the positive law. It is true that in Germany, contrary to the practice in France, the philosophy of law has never been limited to philosophers; jurists have been concerned for quite a long time with *Naturrecht* (natural law) and from early on they have given it more of a positive form. However, while ideal law and real law were supposed to have different origins (the former was a logical consequence of the transcendent human destiny and the latter was constructed for the needs of practical life), the interplay of the two was conceived somewhat artificially, and this was not very productive.

The movement whose origins we have been discussing was naturally bound to accentuate this trend and to make it more explicit by giving it a rationale. The philosophy of law, which just recently came into contact with the science of law, was coming more and more to pervade it. In 1878, G. Jellinek, professor of the faculty of law in Vienna, published a work whose title indicates its spirit: *The Significance of Law, Illegal Acts and Punishment from the Perspective of Social Morality.*[23] But above all one must go to the two enormous volumes that Rudolf von Jhering, Professor at

---

23. G. Jellinek, *Socialethiche Bedeutung von Recht, Unrecht und Strafe,* Vienna, 1878. A study of this book belongs more in a work on criminology in Germany, however.

Göttingen,[24] has published on *The Purpose of Law* to find the new conception of the philosophy of law.[25]

The following passage indicates very clearly the general lines of the proper method to apply to ethics henceforth:

> The old philosophical concept of ethics made it a branch of psychology and a twin sister of logic; the Christian theological concept made it a branch of theology and a twin sister of dogmatics. Our concept makes it a branch of social science and a twin sister of all those disciplines which, like it, are based on the solid ground of social historical experience—that is to say jurisprudence, statistics, political economy and politics. In this way, access to ethics is open to representatives of these different specialties; they can not only enrich it by furnishing it with valuable material that they bring from their own science, but can even assist its progress by bringing to it individual concepts which rightly belong to these special studies. . . .
>
> Furthermore, the number of disciplines that are in a position to offer a helping hand to ethics is not in any way limited to these that I have just mentioned, I am myself prepared to use others for the objectives that I have in mind. First, there is the science of language which I hope to be able to show, by a number of examples, to be highly useful for the analysis of moral ideas. Then there is mythology; along with etymology it is the oldest and most certain witness that we can consult on people's first moral ideas. These two sciences together form something of a paleontology of ethics. . . . From another point of view, another discipline, pedagogy, is called upon to render an important service to ethics, as we shall see when we deal with the question of

---

24. [Rudolf Jhering (Ihering), (1818–1892, Professor of Law at the University of Göttingen, led the revolt against legal positivism by developing a theory of the law based upon its social purpose. His most influential work, *Der Zweck im Recht* (1877), translated into English in 1924 (*Law as a Means to an End*), advanced a theory of social utilitarianism. A pioneer of sociological jurisprudence, Jhering was concerned with the legal aspects of the social problems of industrialization.]

25. Rudolf Jhering, *Der Zweck im Recht,* Leipzig. Vol. 1, second edition, appeared in 1884; 570 pages. The second volume, 722 pages in Octavo, was published in 1886. The work is still unfinished.

the formation of the moral will. . . . When, by the introduction
of all these new elements which its sister sciences make available
and by the application of the empirical historical method which,
without letting itself be abused by preconceived ideas, examines
the facts of the moral order with as much impartiality as the
naturalist examines natural phenomena; when, I say, the ethics
of the future will have in this way resolved the empirical part
of its problem, then the professional philosopher will be able
to come in and create synthesis.[26]

This passage itself shows the author's point of view. He speaks
of law and morality as a jurist. His book is entirely dominated
by an idea which is, to be sure, expressed with more abundance
than precision or depth, but which is therefore all the more instructive
for moral philosophers.

Since the time of Socrates, philosophers have had the habit
of reducing reality to a set of concepts; they think they can explain
the life of the individual as well as that of society by reducing
it to a system of abstract ideas logically connected. By proceeding
in this manner, however, they only perceive the general frameworks
within which events happen; the driving force eludes them. To live
is not to think, it is to act; and the stream of our ideas only reflects
the flow of events which continually runs through us. "If one were
to give a stone the ability to think, this would not make it any
less a stone; all that would have changed is that the external world
would be reflected in it like the moon on the surface of the water."
To live is essentially to affirm one's existence by an act of personal
power (*aus eigener Kraft*). It is the image of a goal that brings
about action. The final cause is the chief motive of our behavior;
there is thus only one way to explain the facts of the internal life
and that is to show its goal. It is naturally the same for social
life; since law is a sociological phenomenon, to give an account
of it one must seek its goal. To explain a rule of law is not to
prove that it is there, but to show that it is of use for something,
that it is well adapted to the purpose it ought to fill (*richtig*). "Correct

26. Rudolf Jhering, *Der Zweck im Recht*, Leipzig, 1884, Vol. II, pp.
124–28.

appropriation (*Richtigkeit*) is the standard of practice as truth is the standard of theory."[27]

One can certainly reproach Jhering for not having studied the concept of the goal very thoroughly. Most often he seems to mean the conscious representation of the end, or at least of one of the ends of conduct. If this is the sense of the term, there exists a class of our actions from which any representation of an end is absent. How often do we act without knowing the goal we intend! The experiences of posthypnotic suggestion have shown new examples of this old observation of Spinoza's. To explain how these sorts of unconscious adaptations happen, one must go beyond consciousness and study the nature of this obscure and diffuse intelligence which plays no small role in the direction of our lives— the operation of feelings, propensities, instincts, habits, their effect on our behavior, and the way they change when circumstances require. These analyses are completely absent from Jhering's book, which in fact seems to recognize only the subjective method in psychology. Furthermore, the notion that all of our actions have conscious goals is highly contestable. There occur in societies, as in individuals, mutations which have causes but no ends, somewhat analogous to Darwin's individual variations. One can find among these variations some that might be useful, although their utility had not been foreseen and was not their determining cause. However, despite the importance of these reservations, one can say in a general way with the author that social phenomena derive from practical causes. To replace Jhering's somewhat metaphysical expression with more scientific language, we might say that every act of human behavior, whether individual or social, has as its object the adaptation of the individual or the society to its environment. No doubt there are actions which serve no purpose, which are adapted to nothing; but if they persist and above all if they become widespread, one can be nearly certain that they were useful or have become so. At least this is the most likely hypothesis and must be tried before all others.

What then is the practical cause that has produced the law?

---

27. Rudolf Jhering, *Der Zweck im Recht,* Leipzig, 1884, Vol. I, p. 437.

It is, says the author, the need to secure the conditions of existence of society (*die Sicherung des Lebensbedingungen des Gesellschaft*). But it is necessary to give the term "conditions" a very broad meaning. "Conditions" cannot mean only those indispensable for survival pure and simple, but everything without which existence would seem to us to be without value. Honor is not a necessary condition of life, but what person with any spirit or what people would want life without honor? Law rests, then, on both objective and subjective causes at once. It is not only relative to the physical environment, to the climate, the number of inhabitants, etc., but even to preferences, to ideas, to the normal culture of a nation. This is why it is changeable and why something is required in one place and prohibited in another. Pascal was right: "Truth on one side of the Pyrenees is error on the other." But truth is not involved here and would not be compromised by all these variations. For once more the law is neither true nor false; it is either appropriate or inappropriate to the aim which is its *raison d'être*.

But someone will ask whether regulations concerning stamps, customs, currencies, etc., are a part of the law; should one see necessary conditions of social life in them? This objection confuses the end with the means. To live it is necessary to eat, but not to eat this or that food. Similarly, for the state to fulfill its functions it must procure the necessary resources, but it is not necessary for it to extract them in this way or that, by a tax on tobacco, alcohol, or stamps. All these detailed measures have a legal character, but a derived one. To see this one must consider not the things themselves, but the relationship to the ends they embody.

However, all the conditions of existence of a society do not necessarily give rise to legal provisions. If the actions that social welfare requires are enough in agreement with personal interests that one could leave the care of accomplishing them to egoism alone, the law would not intervene. Thus we ordinarily have no need of being constrained to preserve our lives, to perpetuate the race, to work, or to exchange the products of our labor. But it can happen that in exceptional cases the natural tendencies do not fulfill their duties: there are suicides, celibacy, begging, strikes, takeovers, etc. When society suffers from these evils, it protects itself and combats them by means of the law. In exceptional cases it replaces the internal power that fails with an external and mechanical pressure. Jhering is thus led to distinguish three types of conditions that are necessary for the existence of societies: first, those that are outside the law (*die ausser rechtlichen Bedingungen*); second, those that rely on the law partly, but only accidentally (*die Gemischt rechtlichen*); and third, those that can only be realized through law (*die rechtlichen*).

One need not believe, however, that in the sphere in which society does not ordinarily intervene, the individual exercises rights that derive from his or her nature and belong only to it. The law is the heavy hand of society on the individual, and where it ceases to make itself felt, rights do not exist.

> There is not one right, even the most private, about which I could say, 'That belongs entirely to me and I am its lord and master.' It is society that has granted all the rights that I possess and it can, if necessary, limit and restrict them. My children are only mine under certain conditions; my fortune is only mine with explicit reservations. If I squander it foolishly, the law intervenes and withdraws its administration from me.

If there is one right which seems to be uniquely instituted with a view to the individual, it is certainly the right to property. This is, in fact, what is taught in the schools. Jhering shows without difficulty how little this theory corresponds to the facts. Are not the laws of accession, of requisition, of expropriation, and the easements which are often imposed upon me without my consent just so many violations of this supposedly inviolable right? Every day the interference of the law in the sphere of private interest becomes greater. People are amazed by it, they complain, and denounce the abuse of regulations and state socialism; but this is because they judge the facts according to an *a priori* principle and an abstract ideal which does not fit reality.

Higher animals have more complicated nervous systems than inferior animals; similarly, as societies grow and become more intricate, the conditions of their existence become more numerous and more complex. This is why civil codes noticeably expand. Things that once seemed to be a luxury are necessary today and imposed by society upon its members: this is the case, for example, with military service and elementary education. It even seems to the author that the circle of life that is strictly individual may be continually narrowing and that the old Roman law might have been more respectful of personal liberty than ours. In this form Jhering's statement is, to be sure, absolutely false. With progress, human beings distinguish themselves more and more from the physical and social world which surrounds them and develop a stronger sense of themselves: the liberty which they enjoy increases at the same rate as their social obligations. This is an obscure and apparently contradictory phenomenon, which, to our knowledge, has not yet been explained. Social progress has two sides which seem to exclude one another, although most of the time we see only one of them. It is certain, however, that the action of the state spreads further and further and that it is not possible to assign a definite limit to it once and for all.

This theory comes into conflict, it is true, with the natural law doctrine according to which the sole function of law is to protect individuals from one another. It represents society as a vast menagerie of wild beasts which the legislator holds at a distance from one another and confines to their respective cells in order to prevent them from devouring one another. But the natural law theorists misunderstand the true nature of society and forget that it cannot be reduced to a mass of citizens, nor can the social interest be reduced to the sum of individual interests. Moreover, even if one holds to this entirely negative definition of the law, it is not difficult to deduce some quite positive consequences from it. Individuals are not separated from their fellow creatures by an abyss, rather they are all so crowded in upon one another that one of them cannot stir in any way without all the others feeling it. There is not one of our actions that does not affect someone's interest, that could not harm someone, and consequently that could not become the object of legislative measures. With respect to Mill's theory, Jhering quite rightly says that he is able to reduce individual liberty to nothing or close to nothing. It is thus only with the help of a common scholastic argument that Mill succeeds in avoiding the consequences of his principle and in reconciling his doctrine with the prescriptions of positive law which no society can do without.

Such is the purpose of the law. The means by which it is realized is constraint. One can say that on this point all the moral theorists of the school we are studying are unanimous: all make constraint the external mark of the law. But there are all sorts of constraints: there are those that one individual exercises over another, those that are exercised in a diffuse way by the whole of a society in the form of mores, customs and public opinion, and those that are set up and concentrated in the hands of the state. It is the last that ensure the effectiveness of the law. Where there is no constraint present, there is no law; and where constraint is less well established, furthermore, the law is less stable. This is what now keeps international law in the state of incoherence and confusion from which it will not emerge for some time.

Not only is force the inseparable companion of law, it is from force that law has emerged. Originally, law was nothing other than force limiting itself in its own interest. In the physical world and also among primitive people, when two forces clash, the conflict only ends through the destruction of the weaker. But it did not take long for people to realize that it was often more economical not to push for the complete annihilation of the adversary; from this arose the institutions of slavery, contracts, and peace treaties, the first forms of law. Every treaty is, in effect, an order that puts a limit on the power of the conqueror: true, it is the conqueror who imposes it upon himself or herself, but it constitutes no less of a law for the benefit of the conquered. So in principle it is force that is essential and the law that is only secondary.

Today the relationship of these two terms is the reverse; force is only the auxiliary, only the servant of the law. But one cannot judge the past by the present. Moreover, it can happen even now that the old relationship between law and force might be temporarily reestablished; that force, instead of allowing itself to be ruled by law, might overthrow the law and create a new one. This is what happens in a *coup d'état* or revolution; and this use of force cannot

be systematically condemned in the name of an abstract principle.
The law is not something sacred in itself, it is a means to an end.
It is only of value if it fulfills its function well, that is, if it assures
the life of society. What if it does otherwise? Then it would be
quite natural for force to intervene and resume for a moment the
place it once had. *Primum Vivere.*

In brief, according to Jhering, the law is "all the conditions
of existence of a society assured by means of external constraint
through the force at the disposal of the state."[28]

Despite the title of his book, Jhering is not content with determining only the purpose of the law; he also seeks the motives
that impel people to respect it. The most general and most powerful
motive is self-interest, and it is to this that the constraint exercised
by the state is primarily addressed. But this is not enough. If the
whole legal order rested only on fear, society would be nothing
but a prison where people only move when they see the whip raised
above them. For society to be possible there must be some unselfish
feelings in us. These tendencies, of which the two principle types
are love (*die Liebe*) and the sense of duty (*das Pflichtgefuhl*), surpass
the domain of law and belong to the domain of pure morality
(*die Sittlichkeit*) without which the law could not endure. Thus,
going beyond the framework he had set out for himself, Jhering
is led to sketch out a whole theory of morality. Its exposition begins
with the second volume and is to be continued in the third which
has not appeared yet. One can, however, trace its general lines
even now.

Morality has the same purpose as the law: it, too, has the
function of assuring social order. This is why, like the law, it consists
of prescriptions that constraint makes obligatory when needed. But
this constraint does not consist of external, mechanical pressure,
it has a more intimate and psychological character. It is not the
state that exercises it, but the whole of society. The force which
is necessary for it is not concentrated in any clearly defined hands
but is disseminated throughout the nation. It is nothing more than
the authority of public opinion which no one, whether high or

---

28. Rudolf Jhering, *Der Zweck im Recht,* Leipzig, 1884, Vol. I, p. 511.

low on the social scale, can escape. Since it is not fixed in precise formulas, morality is more flexible and more free than the law. This is necessarily the case. The state is too gross a mechanism to regulate such complex movements of the human heart. The moral constraint exercised by public opinion, moreover, does not allow itself to be impeded by any obstacle; subtle as air, it penetrates everywhere—"the family hearth as much as the steps of the throne." Law differs from morality not only in its external characteristics, then, but by intrinsic differences as well, although in the current state of Jhering's work one cannot yet clearly see what these are. All that one can say is that morality extends far beyond the law. The actions that it commands us to perform do not have the same claim as those the law prescribes. In a word, law is the minimal morality absolutely necessary for society to endure.

Having demonstrated these principles in a general way, Jhering undertakes to establish them inductively. This part of the book is entirely original; a great number of facts are marshalled in support of the thesis. The author first investigates language and shows, after a long analysis which can hardly be summarized, that it supports his theory.[29] He distinguishes two, not including the law which he has already considered: mores and morality proper.

In defining mores, he thinks they should be distinguished from fashions, and he is thus led to a rather ingenious theory. Most often one attributes fashions to motives that are entirely individual, like the love of change or a taste for finery. But this explanation is not right since these motives are eternal while fashion, characterized by its capricious instability, is a quite recent phenomenon. Its real cause is social: it is due to the need which the upper classes have to distinguish themselves externally from the lower classes. Since the latter tends continually to imitate the former, styles spread contiguously through society. But once a fashion has been adopted by everyone, it loses all its value; it is thus doomed by its own nature to renew itself endlessly.

Having no origin other than the vanity of the classes, fashion

---

29. Rudolf Jhering, *Der Zweck im Recht,* Leipzig, 1884, Vol. II, pp. 15–95.

is thus outside of morality. But it is not the same with customs which are useful supports and often indispensable to morality. These two notions certainly are not synonymous; one can act contrary to custom without offending morality. The actions that custom dictates are not good in themselves, but only because they have the effect of making other actions that are morally wrong impossible or very difficult. They are preventive measures intended not to combat evil but to forestall it; they have a prophylactic character. If it is contrary to custom for a young woman to go out alone at night, it is because at that time her virtue is more in danger. In a word, what custom forbids is not evil in itself but dangerous: customs are to morality as the security guard is to the law. The moral value of customs is real but derived; and in case of any conflict with morality, it is custom that must give way. The author verifies these general propositions with a detailed analysis of customs which takes up no less than 450 pages of the second volume and which is to be continued in the subsequent volume which has not yet appeared. There we will also find the theory of morality proper.

Such is the plan of a work which seems to be all but unknown in France, although it has created something of a stir in Germany. Certainly, we could have a number of reservations. Jhering's psychology is really quite simplistic. Although he is not a utilitarian, he gives calculation and self-interest an inordinate role in the formation of moral ideas and seems to ignore the fact that since the beginnings of human evolution there have been other human drives that are equally powerful. Finally, as is the habit with jurists, he attaches an exaggerated importance to the external form of things. But despite all these objections, Jhering nonetheless deserves credit for being conscious of and clearly indicating the way in which the study of morality can become a real science. The chapter in which he demonstrates the methodology suitable for the "ethics of the future" is excellent. His book is an interesting effort to bring together the philosophy of law and the positive law. Moreover, he has rendered ethics a great service by definitively integrating the study of customs into it. This is an idea that Wilhelm Wundt has just revived, and we shall now see what he does with it.

Part III

The Moral Philosophers
Wilhelm Wundt

The scholars we have mentioned up to this part were only moral philosophers inadvertently; they explored only those aspects of ethics that touched upon their own special sciences. It was natural, however, that this movement would produce a study of the whole of the moral life. This is, in effect, what Alexander Von Oettingen attempted to do some time ago in his *Moral Statistics*.[30] This work contains a great number of facts, useful analyses and statistical data; but the author is a Professor of Theology at the University of Dorpat, so despite the empirical character of the method he employs, the book is still too much of a theological work. This project has recently been taken up by Wilhelm Wundt.[31] His *Ethics* presents a synthesis of all the isolated perspectives and special studies we have considered. So we shall dwell on him for some time.

---

30. Alexander Oettingen, *Die Moralstatistik und die christliche Sitten-lehre: Versuch einer Socialethik auf empirischer Grundlage.* 2 Vols. Erlangen, 1858–1874.

31. [Wilhelm Wundt (1832–1920), known as the founder of experimental psychology, was Professor of Philosophy at the University of Leipzig. While his work on physiological and social psychology was largely unprecedented, his efforts to base philosophical principles on empirical psychology were less successful. Durkheim saw Wundt primarily as a moral philosopher rather than a psychologist, although he admired Wundt's establishment of the first experimental psychology laboratory and was probably influenced by this model in his own establishment of the *Année Sociologique* group. By the 1880s Wundt was, in fact, more of a philosopher, having published voluminous works on logic, ethics and systematic philosophy.]

Wundt's methodology is clearly empirical. There is no philosophical science, he says, in which pure speculation is more un-
productive than in ethics. The complexity of facts here is such
that all systems constructed by reason alone seem utterly inadequate
and crude when one compares them with reality. Reason itself,
furthermore, is mistaken in believing that it is the sole creator of
these brilliant constructions! Far from being adequate to the task,
reason alone cannot cope with the subject and, without knowing
it, borrows from experience all that it thinks it alone has created.

In ethics as elsewhere, one must begin with observation. But
since there are so many facts that attract the observer's attention,
the empirical method has led in rather contrary directions, according
to whether preference is given to this or that type of phenomenon.
As a result, there are as many different ethical theories as there
are different aspects of moral facts. One theorist, for example, makes
the whole of morality consist of the motives that govern our will,
the nature of our intentions. Others, on the contrary, have studied
more the objective consequences of actions and have reflected on
material they have drawn sometimes from the law, sometimes from
political economy, sometimes from the history of civilizations. Thus
a legal ethics is developed, or an economic ethics, or an anthropo-
logical ethics, etc.

Wundt reacts against this tendency which fragments ethics into
an infinity of distinct sciences that ignore one another. He proposes
to show the connections between these special studies and finally
to restore the unity of practical action which this extreme specialization ignores and endangers. He does not conceal the difficulties
of such an undertaking and acknowledges at the outset that it will
necessarily be less than perfect: but he considers it useful to make
the effort.

He even pushes his eclecticism further, attempting to reconcile
not only the diverse directions of the empirical method, but the
empirical method itself with the speculative method. No doubt one
must begin by observing the facts that experience gives us; but
when this is done the problem of ethics is not entirely resolved.
The object of ethics is above all to establish general principles of
which moral facts are only particular applications. The empiricists

believe, it is true, that they can find these principles in certain psychological phenomena; but then they have to limit themselves to an entirely subjective ethical theory. It is hardly likely, however, that such a morally complex world would allow so simple an explanation. Certainly one has no right to decide *a priori* that psychological observation will be insufficient and, as long as we have not come to such a point in science where this inadequacy has become self-evident and we feel the need other procedures, we must reserve judgment and maintain complete impartiality. However, one can expect that what is true for the natural sciences will also hold for ethics. The natural sciences also produce axioms—hypotheses that are not the raw products of experience but are added to it by the mind to make it intelligible. Even though the discovery of such principles must proceed by the observation of facts, still they do not result from observation, but are the product of speculation. The speculation that Wundt has in mind, however, does not consist of any sort of revelation of transcendent truth. It does not oppose observation, but complements it. As long as in explanations we have at our disposal concepts which abstraction and induction have derived directly from experience, observation rules unchallenged. Speculation only begins where these sorts of conceptions fall short and where the mind, under the influence of the need for coherence, which is the real law of thought, creates hypothetical concepts to make experience intelligible. Thus defined, the speculative method is not an exclusively philosophical discipline; rather there is no science that can do without it.

Wundt's method follows the natural divisions of science. It is necessary, first, to look at the facts to see how our present morality is constituted; then to reduce it to its general principles; finally to ask how these principles ought to be applied in the different domains of the moral life. But to these three parts, Wundt adds a fourth. It seems to him that a certain type of preparation is necessary before moving from facts to principles. He fears that in being applied to such an enormous mass of facts, scientific thought would find itself overwhelmed and would simplify the facts artificially. To attain a more comprehensive synthesis, therefore, the better way is to proceed with a comparative study of the different moral theories that have succeeded one another historically from antiquity to the present. The doctrines of theorists are thus to be treated as events in the formation of moral ideas. A critical examination of the major systems of ethics, therefore, forms the second part of Wundt's work.[32]

Psychology cannot tell us how moral ideas are formed and developed, for it knows nothing of this. If morality has its basis in a psychological fact, it terminates in a social fact. It sinks its roots into the heart of the individual, but to discover these roots one must first observe the more elevated branches, then follow all of their bends to see at what point and how they break away from the stem, and retrace this slowly until one finds the trunk from which all this growth comes. To proceed otherwise, to be content with psychological observation alone, would be to close one's eyes voluntarily to what makes morality distinct; it would be to reduce it intentionally to an event of the individual consciousness; and this would be to establish individualism from the outset.

There is only one way to understand collective phenomena, that is to study them in themselves. In other words, it is social psychology (*die Völkerpsychologie*) that alone can furnish the moral theorist with the materials he or she needs; this, according to Wundt, is the gateway (*die Vorhalle*) to ethics. It is in the history of language, of religion, of customs, of civilization in general that we can discover the traces of this development of which individual consciousness contains and knows only the initial impulses.

Four principal factors give birth to morality: (1) religion, (2) customs, (3) the physical environment and (4) civilization in general. But the first two have been by far the most important.

RELIGION

It is no more right to conceive of religion as emerging from morality than morality from religion. In the beginning, law, morality and religion were combined in a synthesis from which it is impossible

---

32. We will have very little to say about the second part and the fourth.

to dissociate the elements. None of these phenomena is prior to any other; but they have successively extricated themselves from this undifferentiated mix in which they had existed in a state of germination. For a long time both legislative power and responsibility for keeping watch over morality were functions that belonged to the priest. We have a striking example of this primitive mixture in the Decalogue where one finds all together commandments concerning the respect of the Sabbath, the respect of life, and of others' property. The Decalogue shows a slight tendency toward differentiation as well since the first five commandments are ethico-religious orders while the last five are really legal prescriptions.

Since morality and religion are blended at this point, there must be some common traits between them. What then is religion? To respond to this question one could begin by studying the religions of primitive people, since they are more simple; one might thus hope to be able to disentangle the essential character of religious phenomena more easily. Unfortunately, by proceeding in this way, mythologists have accepted as simple what was really a complex mixture. Primitive mythology is a mix of all sorts of heterogeneous elements. One finds metaphysical speculations on the nature and order of things, which sometimes made religion into a sort of naive metaphysic. One also finds private as well as public rules of conduct, and this is why certain philosophers consider religion a moral and social discipline. All such theories mistake religion for the different phenomena with which it is involved. To escape this error one must study it among civilized people where it is separated from all the chance elements with which it was formerly united. It is only then that, looking back at primitive religion, one will have any chance of discerning the seeds of these ideas and feelings that the higher religions give us in an advanced state.

But if one follows this method, one will arrive, according to Wundt, at the following conclusion: "All representations and sentiments which refer to an ideal existence conforming perfectly to the wishes and desires of the human heart are by nature religious."[33]

---

33. Wilhelm Wundt, *Ethik: Eine Untersuchung der Thatsachen und Gesetze des sittlichen Lebens,* Stuttgart, 1886, p. 41.

This ideal varies with time; depending upon the people involved, it can be naive or refined, crude or sublime. But one can be assured that there never has been a people who were entirely without an ideal, however humble, because it answers a need that is deeply rooted in our nature.

One can thus understand the relationship between morality and religion. Surely the religious ideal is far from being a moral ideal just because it is religious; on the contrary, it contains elements that are immoral or amoral. Does not one see people venerating in their gods the worst of human vices? But it is nonetheless true that morality has a tendency to express itself in the form of a religious ideal. In fact, the essential and truly religious element in religion is the conception of divinities who are proposed as models for human imitation and who are regarded at the same time as the defenders of the ideal order which they represent. Morality like religion has a need to personify its ideal and to secure for it the guarantee of sanctions. This is why moral and religious ideas are so closely interlaced in their origins that it is impossible to distinguish them.

It is true that with time the two become separated. But the relationship between morality and religion remains close for another reason. To the extent that morality detaches itself from religion, religion seems to make an effort to draw nearer to morality. Religion modifies and moralizes its concepts so well that it remains a useful auxiliary for ethics. Although the most primitive divinities themselves were somewhat human, thanks to the cult of ancestors, the gods of the natural religions (*Naturreligionen*) more often symbolized entirely physical forces which hardly had any connection with morality or the social order. But little by little the gods, while preserving their superior nature, drew closer to people and became human. The cult of natural forces was replaced by that of heroes who were nothing more than divinized humans. Finally the great monotheistic religions developed which all had this character of being incarnate in humans—Moses, Jesus, Mohammed. Thus the religious ideal disengaged itself step by step from the physical environment, while retaining clear markings of it, in order to become centered in a great human personality and to become truly ethical.

Notions relating to sanctions naturally followed the same evolution; it is no longer accuracy in the observance or omission of religious practices, but ethical merit or demerit that religion rewards or punishes.

Then, if morality was originally merged with religion, little by little it became separated, until eventually religion modeled itself on morality. But morality does not emerge immediately. Between religion and morality proper there is an intermediate step which is custom.

CUSTOMS

We have often viewed customs as simply generalized habits. An individual adopts a way of acting because he or she happens upon it and this is imitated by others eager to profit from the example. The habit presumably spreads step by step among individuals until little by little it becomes collective. But this theory wrongly supposes that the individual is the principal force of social life. Language and religion were not invented one day by someone whose example was followed either voluntarily or by force by his or her fellows. From the fact that collective phenomena do not exist outside the consciousness of individuals, it does not follow that they come from this consciousness; they are rather the work of the community. Collective phenomena do not leave individuals to be spread through society; they rather emanate from society and are then diffused among individuals. Individuals receive them rather than create them, although each has collaborated in their production in an infinitesimally small way.

This is, in effect, why these facts are much too complex to be embraced by a single mind. We never grasp anything immediate but the consequences of our simplest actions; how can we know the distant and obscure effects of phenomena that branch out in every direction through the social organism? The individual, furthermore, is too small to affect society. No doubt the useful habits that he or she initiates are capable of spreading somewhat, but they cannot get beyond a very restricted circle; they can hardly extend beyond the family, the small world of friends, or the corporation. Fashions and common practices also arise in this way. What always distinguishes such practices from customs is that they have no obligatory power. Rather than habits transforming themselves into customs, one often sees customs which diminish in power and fall back into the state of individual habits.

Customs, as collective facts, must have other collective facts for causes. In fact, rather than seeking rationally how it might have been possible for things to happen, if one observes historically how they have actually happened, one will see that all social customs have their origins in other social customs. When the causes that have brought about the formation of a custom have disappeared or have been modified, the custom does not thereby disappear; it persists by virtue of the general law of inertia to which customs, like everything else, are subject. At times it happens that they persist in this way without purpose and without reason, veritable petrifactions of the past. Most often, however, they retain enough flexibility to adapt themselves to other ends and thus to give birth to new customs. In fact, this process is only a metamorphosis. In any case, in the uninterrupted succession of customs which beget one another, we never see the least gap or the smallest joint through which individual initiative can be introduced.

But finally, if we go back from custom to custom, what do we find at the origin? Still more social facts, namely beliefs and religious practices. One might certainly add juridical prescriptions, but since they are indiscernible from religious precepts, the distinction is of no significance. One must understand this correctly. Other moral theorists have recognized that there was once some relationship between social customs and religious ideas; but this relationship seemed to them to be only external and superficial. It seemed to them that customs were generated by private interests and that religion only gave them an external form and the authority of sanctions. For example, if a certain tribe killed their infants as soon as they were born, as some say, because they were too poor to feed them, then this habit, once it arose and was established, took on a religious character.

Wundt rejects this explanation and does not think that customs could arise outside of religion. If primitives kill their infants it is to sacrifice them to the gods, just as they offer the gods the first fruits of all their most precious goods. This is why the sacrificed child is always the eldest of the family. Later, when religious motives disappear, religious practices become social customs. No doubt if they persisted, it was because of nonreligious motives which perhaps came close to those that are commonly given; but they did not owe their origins to these.

Thus one can understand the relationship between customs and morality. Customs are derived from religion and religion contains moral elements which are naturally transmitted to customs. If even those customs that appear most foreign to morality contain some germs of morality, it is religion that has imparted them. If from their origins they have the effect of controlling self-interest and of motivating people to self-sacrifice and unselfishness, it is not because the primitive intellect appreciated the advantages and beauty of altruism. All this happens automatically; customs produce moral consequences without these having been intended or foreseen. Religious feelings bind people to things other than themselves and make them dependent upon superior powers which symbolize the ideal. This unconscious altruism is embodied in practices and remains there even though the religious idea is withdrawn and the practices become customs. It is no doubt modified as they are modified, and adapts itself to new ends which assure its survival. But one need not believe that altruism only appears at that time.

Thus for a long time law and morality were merged with custom, just as in an even earlier epoch custom had been merged with religion. Actually, among primitive tribes there was no written or established law; the nuances by which we distinguish legal prescriptions from those of morality were unknown among them. Both were indiscriminately placed under the sanction of custom which had great power of constraint. The authority of custom was not something vague as it is today; it was quite clear because it was unified. Any departure from custom was met with equally rigorous punishment. Then little by little this homogeneity was broken. Law separated itself from custom and took for itself the means of punishment which until then was the force of custom in general.

From that time on custom retained only internal means of coercion, such as public honor or disgrace with all the degrees these sentiments have.

Custom and morality, however, do not coincide, for there are customs that are morally wrong. Morality (*die Sittlichkeit*) is potential in customs (*die Sitte*), but it is not actual; it is mixed with elements that have nothing to do with ethics. By the term "morality" Wundt means simply the morality of the most civilized nations. The general principles of this morality are set out in the second part of his *Ethics*. At this point it is only a question of how these ideas and beliefs, such as we know and practice them without having any abstract formulation of them, emerge little by little from customs.

MORALITY

From the fact that social customs had their origins in religious practices, it does not follow that in the final analysis moral sentiments are derived solely from religious sentiments. In addition to religious sentiments there were, from the outset, social tendencies that had their origins in human nature. In fact, all people have what amounts to a natural affinity for their equals which became apparent as soon as people began to live together, that is to say, since the first days of humanity. What drew them together with one another was not, as is often said, blood relationship, but similarities of language, habits, and manners. The earliest societies were not families but much more indeterminate aggregates in which ties were not formed based upon parentage. Families only came into existence later; it was the result of a differentiation that eventually occurred within the tribe.

The affinity of like for like (*die Neigung zu dem Genossen*) is thus the earliest form of social inclination. However rudimentary it might be, this sentiment is not a product of egoism. It is, in principle, an autonomous factor of moral progress. But it was so weak, so indefinite, that it would have been quickly overcome by tendencies toward egoism if it had to struggle against them alone.

It found a powerful ally, however, in religious sentiments. Religion, as we have seen, was a natural school of impartiality and self-denial. Respect for divine orders and sympathy for fellow creatures are the two sources from which all our altruistic instincts emerge and with these the whole of morality.

Nonetheless, egoism played a part in this evolution: one finds traces of it in every primitive morality. Altruism was so weak that it could hardly have prevailed even with the assistance of religion if egoism had not lent a hand. One finds in Homer many accounts of unselfish acts; but the motives are always marked by naive egoism. If a warrior risks his life to save another, it is because such devotion is glorious or generally useful since it is a means of acquiring support which one may need.

How, then, do egoistic motives, which are so powerful at the outset disappear from moral conduct and give way to genuinely disinterested motives? Do they become more enlightened? And did people after a while realize that egoism was its own enemy? This would be to attribute a rather extraordinary power of foresight to human intelligence in general and especially to the crude intelligence of primitive peoples. In reality the evolution has been entirely mechanical; neither calculation nor foresight has played any part in it. Egoistic motives eliminated themselves because they were self-contradictory. In other words, evolution is the product of a type of stabilization and of a spontaneous regularization of these sorts of tendencies (*Compensation und Selbstregulation egoistischer Triebe*). Let us imagine that in some instance pure sympathy does not have enough force to prevail over egoistic inclinations and that it can only find support from self-interested motives. When this happens the egoistic satisfaction one feels from having triumphed over oneself can become a motive *sui generis* which reinforces the tendency toward sympathy and assures its victory in the future without any further need for appeal to self-interested considerations. Egoistic factors are thus neutralized and cancel one another, while a genuinely altruistic tendency emerges from the mass that had enclosed it. This altruism, however, is not just a disguised or transformed egoism; and it would be a mistake to confuse its origin with that ascribed to it by the Utilitarians. Altruism does not come from egoism, for nothing can come from its opposite. It rather exists from the beginning obscured, in part, and often neutralized by personal interests. These interests do not give birth to their contraries when they recede; they only cease to obstruct their growth. Furthermore, personal interests are certainly not extinct, nor will they ever disappear entirely. There is room in the human mind for more than one sentiment.

Since this original sympathy attaches itself uniquely to individuals, it naturally varies with them. And history demonstrates that this primitive tendency becomes more and more differentiated in so far as the social contexts in which it appears differ. At first one and the same sentiment unites all the members of a tribe (*Stammgefühl*), and consequently there is just one morality that is common to all—a morality which is as simple or as inconsistent as the society it represents. But when the family begins to emerge from the body of this homogeneous mass, domestic feelings develop and simultaneously domestic morality. Then states are born, classes and casts are organized, inequalities multiply, and collective sentiments as well as morality become diversified in accordance with social conditions. There is a morality for each social class— slaves, free people, priests, warriors, etc. On the other hand, since morality has religious origins, it is national like religion. Each nation has its own morality which pertains only to itself: one only has duties and obligations toward one's fellow citizens.

But this dispersion of moral ideas is not the final word on progress. For a long time a movement toward concentration has been underway which is still going on before our eyes. To the extent to which societies increase in size, the bonds that attach people to one another cease to be personal. Actual sympathy is replaced by a more abstract, but no less powerful, attachment to the community of which one is a part, that is, to the material goods and ideas that people possess in common—art, literature, sciences, customs, etc. From that point on, members of the same society are friends and help one another not just because they know one another, or just to the extent that they know one another, but because they all participate in the collective consciousness. This sentiment is too impersonal to permit morality to have the variety it had formerly; it is too general for morality to remain particular. To the extent that common ideas and sentiments come from the depths of society, differences disappear. Intermingled in the body of the social consciousness that surrounds them, individuals and classes by virtue of their own relationships can see the gaps which once separated them gradually diminish. This fusion of individuals and classes certainly does not make external inequalities disappear. This is neither possible nor desirable, for inequality is a stimulant which, if it is not moral itself, is necessary for morality. It is no less true, however, that all the citizens of the same nation tend more and more to see themselves as equals of one another because they are all servants of the same ideal—whence comes the increasing uniformity of dress, style, manners, etc., and the increasingly pronounced tendency toward the leveling of social inequalities. At the same time, this communal ideal, by being impersonal, is increasingly independent of time and space. It is thus elevated more and more above particular societies to become the sole ideal of humanity. In other words, at the same time that the moralities of class and cast disappear, national moralities also finally disappear to make room for a morality of humanity.

As to civilization, it has a rather complex influence on this tendency. Improvements in the means of transportation and communication have certainly contributed to the acceleration of this movement toward concentration; advances in technology have relieved people of mechanical work which was a crushing weight on the development of the mind; education has spread through classes it had not previously touched, and the state now requires it of citizens. But there are still goods that are unequally apportioned. The speed of communications, by endlessly extending markets and by making individual prosperity dependent upon an infinite number of very complex causes, requires of each of us efforts at forecasting and an expenditure of energy which were formerly unnecessary for life. Finally, the current organization of industry has the effect of separating entrepreneurs more and more from the workers and of reviving slavery in a new form. So in effect civilization is not a moral factor by itself; it contains elements of all sorts and has for morality as many disadvantages as advantages.

Of course, this is no reason to hold humanity back—as ridiculous an undertaking as it is absurd—for the world moves unalterably forward and it is impossible to prevent change. If civilization has its imperfections and its dangers, one must simply take them in hand and try to get rid of them.

This historical analysis of moral ideas which occupies almost half of Wundt's work can be summarized as follows:

The Elements of Morality[34]

The elements common to all concepts of morality are the following:

Formal Elements

The idea of morality is expressed universally in the form of antithetical concepts to which judgments of approval and disapproval are attached. The things to which people attach positive moral value are those that bring lasting satisfaction. This idea of duration is expressed in the form of religious beliefs concerning immortality.

Material Elements

Since moral ideas include elements that reappear in every period of history, these elements must consist of certain psychological facts that are derived from human nature in general, for human nature alone remains everywhere the same through the extreme instability of historical change. In fact we have seen that the whole moral life was transformed by two great tendencies: the inclination toward sympathy and the sentiment of respect (*die Ehrfurchts- und die Neigungsgefühle*). The second of these sentiments comes from religious beliefs; the first from social life. But little by little they were combined in a thousand ways and from these combinations comes the whole complex of moral ideas.

---

34. [This summary is found at the end of Vol. I of Wundt's *Ethics.*]

GENERAL LAWS OF MORAL EVOLUTION

The Law of the Three Stages

The first appearances of moral life show a very great homogeneity; social tendencies are simple and very weak. In the second period social sentiments are differentiated and produce a spontaneous differentiation of moral ideas (*die Trennung der sittlichen Begriffe*). Finally, the third stage is the age of synthesis and concentration.

The Law of the Heterogeneity of Ends
(*Das Gesetz der Heterogenie der Zweche*)

This is the most general principle of moral evolution and the one to which the author seems to attach the most importance. Voluntary actions produce consequences that surpass the motives that caused them. When we become conscious of consequences that we did not foresee, they become the object of new actions and give rise to new motives. These in turn produce effects which again extend beyond them and so on indefinitely. One can then establish the principle that the results of our actions are never the real motives; and for the same reason one can be assured that the motives which inspire our action today are not those that originally produced it. When a body falls into a quiet pool of water, one sees a circular wave form on the surface which then gives rise to a larger one that surrounds it. At the same time the first one spreads and seems to try to overtake the second; but before it can catch it, the second moves further along, and then a third wave is formed which in turn moves away when the second tries to join it. Moral ideas develop is the same way. The results of our actions always spread beyond their motives and to the extent that motives approach them, they move further away.

This law sheds a great deal of light on the evolution of morality in the future. By making us aware of how limited our ability to predict is, it takes from us the right to set a logical limit to evolution. Theory is always inadequate to reality. We must renounce speculation concerning the end of our efforts, since even the next goal escapes us. All that we can do is to outline beforehand and in very general terms the direction the future will take. We must be careful not to confine ethical ideals to the narrow circle of our immediate hopes and desires. On the contrary, the particular should be seen as a form of the universal (*Das Einzelne will betrachtet sein sub specie aeternitatis*).

To summarize, then, moral ideas are formed under the influence of unconscious causes the consequences of which they conceal. Deliberate thought plays only a small part in this process; it only intervenes to establish and consecrate results that came about without conscious thought. Religion spontaneously gives rise to customs, and customs, in turn, to morality. This theory is analogous to the way Darwin explained the formation of instincts, moral or otherwise. In effect, for this English theorist, instincts result from accidental variations that are found to be useful to animals, but which originated without any goal.

It is the same for Wundt: customs originate or are modified under the influence of causes that are quite different from the functions they later fulfill. It is only after they are developed and after we have experienced them that we become conscious of their value. Only then does what was a result become a goal. It is necessary, however, to avoid pressing this similarity too far and seeing a transformationist morality in Wundt's ethic. First, although there is nothing directly proportionate between moral ideas and their original causes, there is nonetheless some relationships between them. If morality comes from religion, it is because religion, like morality but in another way, is an expression which approximates the ideal. If the pure love of humanity is gradually separated from the cruder sentiments which once shared a place with it in the human heart, it is because it had this potential. For Darwin, on the contrary, there is no relationship at all between the causes which produce accidental variations in the organism and the reasons that stabilize them in the species.

On the other hand, according to Darwin and Spencer, what determines the survival of these variations is their utility to the individual or to the species. Wundt absolutely refuses to apply the theory of natural selection to morality. Since the struggle for life

is a product of self-interest, it cannot give way to unselfish inclinations. Far from being a product of this struggle, the function
of morality is to ease and regulate it. One can easily see that one
animal prevails over another because it is the stronger. It is hard
to see, however, how self-denial and the spirit of sacrifice could
assure victory. Should one say that people, having become aware
of the dangers of unrestrained egoism, have tried to contain it and
that antisocial characteristics have gradually diminished? Such an
hypothesis fails to recognize the feeble scope of human intelligence
and cannot be reconciled with the law we have just described. The
evolution of morality, then, has not been governed by considerations
of utility properly speaking.

Finally, Darwin and Spencer hypothesize the inheritance of
moral ideas and sentiments. Wundt considers this incredible. "No
doubt," he says,

> one can imagine that in the course of evolution associations might
> be formed between certain elements of the nervous system, and
> that a disposition toward reflex and spontaneous movements
> aimed at a specific end could be transmitted by heredity; in fact
> a number of observations count in favor of this opinion. But
> how moral intuitions could arise from these dispositions of the
> nervous system is and remains a mystery. When there is some
> question of whether data of consciousness as elementary as sim-
> ple sense perceptions or the concept of space are innate to us,
> how can one speak of innate moral intuitions? These intuitions
> require a multitude of complex empirical representations which
> are relative to the agent, to his or her fellow creatures and to
> other relations he or she has with the external world. In fact,
> these purely imaginary conceptions are no closer to real neurol-
> ogy than the voyages of Jules Verne are to astronomy and
> geography.[35]

---

35. Wilhelm Wundt, *Ethik: Eine Untersuchung der Thatsachen und
Gesetze des sittlichen Lebens,* Stuttgart, 1886, pp. 344–45.

ETHICAL PRINCIPLES[36]

This is how the current morality is formed; we now look at the principles on which it rests.

Two polar ideas act as centers of gravity around which ethical theories can be grouped: individualism on the one hand, and universalism on the other. For the individualists, the only reality in the world is the individual and it is to him or her that all is related. Family, country, and humanity are just means of assuring the free development of the individual. Of course, individualists do not all conceive their ideal in the same manner: some think it consists in the greatest possible happiness, others in the harmonious perfection of all our faculties. But all agree that there are only individual ends, however they define them.

Wundt offers a long refutation of these doctrines. We have seen in effect that altruistic sentiments, whatever connections they might have with egoistic sentiments, are not derived from them. Each has its own source in the human heart from which it springs. Just as the solitary individual of which Rousseau dreamed has never existed, so there has never been a human will in which egoism was the only motive. The two tendencies co-exist with one another and with humanity.

A false metaphysical theory has often served as the basis of this individualistic ethic. It represents the self as a transcendent being, an immutable substance which phenomena both conceal and disclose at the same time. Consequently the self is always bound to focus upon itself, unable to break away. Sacrifice and self-denial are impossible because this substantive being cannot give up its essence; the principle of the conservation of energy opposes it.

This metaphysical hypothesis, however, is the product of a false analogy. To be able to conceive of the relationships between material phenomena we must form a concept that permits us to connect one thing with another; and this concept can contain nothing

---

36. [Subheading added—RTH. In Durkheim's analysis this marks the transition to Volume III of Wundt's *Ethics;* the passage just quoted is Durkheim's only reference to Volume II of the work.]

phenomenal since its contents must by definition be inaccessible to the senses. This is the concept of substance. Once this notion is formed, the mind is tempted to apply it by analogy to mental phenomena for which it was not constructed and to which it is not appropriate. Mental states, in effect, are directly known to us and we see immediately how they are connected with no need of recourse to this metaphysical hypothesis. They are only variations of other phenomena; we ascertain this through mental experience. Here the phenomenal reality is itself sufficient; there is nothing to see beyond it.

Consequently, individualism lacks a theoretical basis. If our minds contain only phenomena, then our personalities no longer have clearly fixed limits which make reciprocal penetration impossible. For the content of our consciousness (ideas, feelings, etc.) is something we hold in common with other people, above all with those with whom we are closest such as our parents and our fellow citizens. In this way we are identical to them. In a word, there are in us a whole host of impersonal elements that explain similar feelings.

But for all this, one has no need to think that the human personality disappears in the depths of the collective being of which it is no more than a superficial modification. The will prevents it from being dissolved in the milieu that surrounds it. Once the will is formed, it reacts to all those phenomena which approach it from without and which are the common inheritance of society; it makes them its own. Individual consciousness detaches itself from the community which appeared ready to absorb it, sets itself off in relief from this uniform background, and establishes itself. Each will is, as it were, a center of crystallization around which the ideas and feelings which belong to each of us individually take shape. Historical progress has the effect of constantly extending the circle of internal and personal phenomena. Far from the individual being the primitive fact and society the derived, the former only slowly disengages itself from the latter. But while the life of the individual takes shape and expands, the collective life is not thereby diminished. It becomes all the more rich and self-conscious. The actions of the group, however unconsidered they might be, become voluntary.

The error of universalists like Hegel and Schopenhauer is that they have not seen this aspect of reality. Since they make personality a simple appearance, they cannot attribute any ethical value to it. They do not perceive that while the individual receives so much from society, he or she nevertheless acts upon society. This is most apparent with great figures whose influence universalists of all schools are forced to deny. No doubt the average consciousness borrows more from its milieu than it can return. Still there are people whose personal ability to react is so great that ideas and feelings which formerly were implicit and latent in society become concentrated in them and gather an extraordinary force which brings them to actualization. These people then become the living conscience of society which is itself transformed under their influence. It is to such great minds that the majority of human progress is due. If progress was left to the average mentality, nothing would change; since the average mentality is passive, it has neither the need nor the means to throw off the yoke of tradition and prejudice. Fortunately these powerful wills appear from time to time like great disturbing forces which keep the present from being like the past and the future from resembling the present.

Moreover, if this personal influence is evident primarily with great figures, one can see it elsewhere to a lesser degree. If great personalities are needed to move the enormous societies of today, lesser personalities can stir the smaller societies which comprise the larger—like the family, the community, the corporation, etc. Thus at all levels of the social scale, it is the individual will which is the source of social change. Morality, therefore, must have a place both in the part and in the whole, both in the individual and in society. One must not lose sight of this principle when one investigates the goals, motives, and norms of moral behavior.

Ethical Goals

To determine the goals of ethics it is not necessary to begin by defining the moral ideal for the purpose of deducing specific goals as the Utilitarians and Rationalists do. This would be to place an arbitrary and suspect hypothesis at the foundation of the science.

One should rather observe human actions carefully and note the purposes of those which the general consciousness recognizes as moral. And since our behavior concerns either ourselves, or society, or humanity, the goals of our actions are either individual, social or human.

When one directs one's efforts toward oneself, the intended goal amounts to one thing, self-preservation. But everyone agrees that there is nothing moral about self-preservation for its own sake. Life has no value on its own; it is only valued accordingly to the use one makes of it. It is only a means to an end. This object can be individual or general. In the second case the action is ethical: it is good to survive in order to preserve oneself for one's family, or for one's country, or for humanity. But if the goal is personal, one must distinguish whether the agent has in mind happiness or perfection. Does one seek his or her happiness only in the pursuit of egoistic goals? Does one work to perfect himself or herself only for a self-seeking purpose? If so, one's behavior is not a matter of ethical value. If, on the contrary, someone takes delight in serving others, if it is for the general good that someone seeks perfection, everyone finds this person's behavior good and approves. In short, individual goals only have moral value if they serve as the means to general goals. The personality of the agent, in any case, cannot be the real object of ethical action.

Does it follow that ethical action can have as its object the personality of someone else? This would be even less rational, for what can have no ethical value for oneself can have none for anyone else. No doubt we admire charity even when it is only a private virtue. But it is not in charity itself that the moral good we ascribe to it resides; for if there is no merit in seeking my own happiness, there can be no more in seeking someone else's. These sorts of actions are only of interest as indications: they reveal a tendency on the part of the agent to sacrifice his or her private interests to external goals. These external goals, which alone can confer an ethical character on behavior, are public welfare and general progress. And this does not mean just the welfare of the greatest number or the progress of the majority. For if the happiness and the perfection of the individual do not constitute ethical goals, neither can the happiness and perfection of thousands of individuals. The addition of zeros cannot increase it.

Ethics must rather be a question of the welfare and progress of society considered as a being that has its own life and personality. The whole, as we have seen, is something more than the sum of its parts, and ethics is a matter of the whole. Under these circumstances sacrifice has significance and is attractive. In order for one to have the right to ask a person to subordinate his or her personal goals to those of others, these goals must be of a higher nature as is the case with collective goals. If the individual does not play the primary role in ethics, it is because he or she is too small to matter: what does his or her suffering or joy mean to the world? It is a drop of water in the sea of life. An ephemeral being, he or she lives only in the present.

Societies, on the other hand, are immersed in the past and extend toward the future: this is why they are more worthy objects of our love and devotion. But the interest we have for the different social groups of which we are a part is not equal; it varies with their size. We are interested in the future of our children and grandchildren, but the futures of our great-grandchildren leave us more indifferent. The notion that our country may cease to exist in a few generations is quite distressing, but this prospect is much more bearable if it is moved off a few thousand years. Finally there is a thought to which we cannot bring ourselves at all; it is that even in thousands and thousands of years the whole of humanity might disappear without leaving a trace in the world.

For this reason human goals alone are truly ethical. As to the others they only have value as provisional incarnations of the common ideal of humanity. Clearly, this ultimate goal of all our efforts can contain nothing particular; it can have as its object only the universal spirit of humanity and can only inspire intellectual efforts of an entirely general scope (*allgemeine geistige Schöpfungen*). One will find the definition of it imprecise; in fact, the human ideal cannot be defined. Any definition simply conveys the fact that no particular expression of the human ideal can definitively satisfy the ethical feelings of humanity. Each forward step that humanity takes pushes the ideal further than humanity can itself foresee; new progress gives rise to new needs. The concept that humanity has of this ideal will thus never be realized; the task it has before it is limitless. To raise oneself to consciousness of the ideal is to separate the object of ethics from all conditions of time and space that make it particular, and to embrace it in all its universality and infinity. Only a few exceptional minds have ever attained this lofty concept. Only extraordinary people like Moses, Socrates or the Christ have known how to live for all times and places, and this is why their actions have left traces which will not disappear as long as humanity has a history. As to average people, they only act with a view to the most immediate goals; their vision hardly extends past the little worlds in which they live.

Such is the goal of ethics, the purpose of morality. But what are the motives that impel us to realize it? One must remember that the two are separate questions.

Ethical Motives

Every motive is a feeling, and every feeling is conditioned by a mental image and varies according to the type of image that conditions it. At times this consists simply of a sense perception which immediately elicits a feeling with no room for reflection or calculation. For example, the sight of a person in danger immediately raises in us a feeling of compassion which incites us to offer help. Wundt calls these "motives of perception" (*Wahrnehmungsmotiven*). They can be divided into two principle types: the sense of oneself or personal dignity, and sympathy (*das Selbstgefühl; das Mitgefühl*).

When what is to be done is not clear, however, or when there is a conflict among our obligations, things do not happen this quickly. Between the image and the feeling a whole chain of logically connected images intervenes—a deliberation of some length. New feelings arise which are the result not of an instantaneous perception of things, but of a consciousness of the collateral consequences of action. These can also be divided into two types which correspond to those mentioned before: personal and collective tendencies (*die eigennützigen und die gemeinnützigen Triebe*). By personal tendencies one means those which have not our happiness for their object, but the full and complete development of our nature. Even with this reservation, however, it is indisputable that these two types of tendencies have unequal importance in morality: the former has much less value than the latter. Both are included in the category of motives of understanding (*Verstandesmotive*), however.

Finally, there are those motives that come from a clear representation not of immediate goals, but of the ultimate goal of human behavior—the ideal destiny of humanity. As a matter of fact, no one can have a precise or definite image of this goal for it extends beyond not only all actual limits, but all intelligible limits. It consists of the anticipation of an indefinite future; to be accurate, it is more of an idea than a mental image. The motives to which it gives rise are called rational (*Vernunftmotive*). They govern action in a way that is as direct as the motives of perception, but in this case the behavior is eminently conscious and reflective. In fact, when the mind attains this serene height, it is no longer aware of the conflicts of duty that perplex the ordinary conscience. Understanding, rather than reason, is the battlefield reserved for these interior conflicts.

These three types of motives are not different in nature, however. There are only differences of degree among them. First, with time and habituation the motives of reason and understanding can become automatic and can be transformed into motives of perception. Nor is this transformation one of degradation; there can be some advantages in ethics to having these set and consolidated in morality. On the other hand, motives of perception and understanding are already rational motives although not consciously so. In effect, every feeling includes and intensifies an infinity of experiences and ideas that the conscious mind does not realize and which only reflective analysis can rediscover and distinguish. When a person risks his or her life for another without thinking, it is because of a more or less clear sense that he or she is one with the person saved. But this connection that unites us with our fellow creatures is only one of the innumerable and invisible connections which put us in closer and closer communication with, and under the domination of, the spirit of humanity. A vague image of the totality of which we are a part, and of the solidarity which binds us there is thus at the base of all the motives. of ethical behavior. This image is obscure and incomplete in the motives of perception and more reflective and precise in the motives of understanding. But it is only in rational motives that it comes to full consciousness of itself. Here the motive coincides with the purpose.

Ethical Norms

Ethical goals have the particular character of being conceived as obligatory. A normal person cannot have them in mind without thinking at the same time that they ought to be realized. In other words, the conception of ethical goals is not a primitive fact of conscience; they rather appear only as derivatives of judgments with an imperative character. Analysis separates and isolates them, but in this state they are only intellectual abstractions. What are really primary and concrete in the ethical life are norms, the prescriptions from which the rest are derived.

How are such imperative judgments possible? People have conceived them as the sovereign orders of a mysterious power which speaks to us and commands us. Whatever form they may have, these explanations are without value today, for they assume that the moral law is immutable and carved in stone from eternity and for eternity even though we know that ethical ideas are subject to evolution. Furthermore, it is a mistake to believe that there must be some entirely special and extraordinary mechanism that permits people to recognize propositions as universal and unconditional. Ethical judgments are not the only ones that have been subject to doubt; there have been and still are many other judgments which now and then have the character of very weak and futile motives. We have here a particular application of the law of the heterogeneity of cause and effect. The obligatory character that marks ethical maxims results from causes which have hardly any relationship to the effects they have produced.

There are, in fact, perfectly intelligible motives that give this authority to ethical goals. They are of four types which differ in degree on an ethical scale. Because of their prescriptive nature,

Wundt calls them imperative motives. First there is the fear of constraint and in particular of external or physical constraint. This is the lowest form of ethical character, but it is sufficient to assure the strict legality of actions. Above this there is the internal ethical constraint that public opinion and the respect we have for it exercises on each of us. These are the two imperatives of constraint (*die Imperative des Zwangs*); much higher than these are the imperatives of liberty (*die Imperative der Freiheit*). The former produce only external signs and symptoms of ethical conduct, the latter have their origin in the conscience of the agent. One of these higher is the lasting satisfaction that ethical action leaves behind. Everything that has been said above demonstrates that this is the effect of virtue. What is evil is that which takes too much interest in the transitory, since whatever is immediate can only be related to passing pleasures. Ethics, however, connects us with what is eternal, and the pleasure that it gives partakes of the permanence of such an objective. Finally there is a later motive, higher than the others, which only the elite can attain. It is a product of the attraction that the contemplation of the ethical ideal alone has. When it attains this fulfillment of itself, ethical consciousness casts aside as useless all the artificial conduct, all the supplemental motives that are of use to mediocre or merely average souls. The cause, in this case, becomes the same as the effect.

This is how the rules that motivate behavior are formed. Those which we find in our conscience and which are, as we have said, the primitive facts of morality are special and particular. The task of the moral philosopher is to condense this incoherent multitude of prescriptions and to reduce them to a few general norms which summarize the whole of ethics. There are, naturally, as many of these fundamental norms as there are ethical goals, i.e., three. But each of these has a double nature and takes two forms according to whether it is directed toward the objective scope of action or the subjective state of the agent. Thus one obtains the following taxonomy:

INDIVIDUAL NORMS
Subjective Form: Thought and action that never lose sight of oneself.

Objective Form: The fulfillment of obligations, whether to oneself or to others, which one imposes on oneself.

SOCIAL NORMS
Subjective Form: Respect for one's neighbor as oneself.
Objective Form: Service to the community to which one belongs.

HUMAN NORMS
Subjective Form: Consideration of oneself as an instrument in the service of the ethical ideal.
Objective Form: Sacrifice of oneself for the goal one recognizes as one's ethical ideal.

CONCLUSION[37]

This analysis, we believe, confirms what we first mentioned: Wundt's work constitutes a proposal for bringing together all those isolated efforts mentioned in Parts I and II above. The teachings of academic socialism, the data of social psychology, and certain of Jhering's views form the basis of this doctrine.

Actually, one senses an influence of a slightly different origin as well. This imposing mass of facts is animated by a breath of idealism which the author attributes to Kant, although it seems to contain nothing uniquely Kantian. For Kant, in fact, the categorical imperative is neither vague nor indeterminate; its commands are very precise and it speaks with equal clarity to the ignorant and to the intelligent. One is reminded more of Fichte than of Kant when Wundt speaks of an indefinite and indefinable moral ideal of which only some rare minds attain consciousness. In any case, whether Wundt's idealism is closer to Kant or to Fichte, there is certainly nothing transcendental or mystical about it. It is not composed of intuitions of the beyond or an escape to infinity, but only of empirical hypotheses. This is a postulate Wundt needs in order to explain the facts. His doctrine takes on a more complex

---

37. [Subheading added—RTH]

form in this way and even a more eclectic character; but it remains an attempt at an experimental ethic despite its perhaps excessive conclusions.

Wundt's perspective marks progress in two ways beyond the earlier moral theories we have discussed. We have seen the influence that most of these moral theorists have attributed to calculation and the human will in the evolution of moral ideas. According to these earlier theories the great institutions of morality and of society have been, at least in part, conscious creations. And if reflection has constructed the social world, it can restructure it; if society is a product of logic, logic can rebuild it. In other words, to know how the social world is made, the mind has only to ask itself how it is engaged in making it; observation is useless, deduction is sufficient. To observe or to experiment is to model our ideas on things; but such a method is only necessary if things do not always follow the laws of understanding. Therefore, although this school of moral theorists can be characterized as having a veritable horror of logical abstractions and a profound feeling for the complexity of facts, still, due to the very large role it attributes to calculation and foresight in social development, it often ends up replacing observation with reasoning and dialectic.

Wundt breaks completely with this rational method. He says repeatedly that it is not a matter of knowing what logically ought to be, but of knowing what is the case. Thus the explanation that Jhering gives of customs and their origins is no longer satisfying; he sees them as useful habits which become increasingly general. According to Wundt, however, it is observation, not reason, that ought to answer this question, and observation tells us that social customs have never been derived from private habits. However strange this may seem, customs have always been produced by other customs or, originally, by religious practices. Logic alone would never have predicted this. Furthermore, Wundt is not content with asserting this disagreement between logic and the facts; he shows the reason for it. He says it is because the motives behind our actions are not in keeping with the ends they produce, and it is the ends which are important because they alone give our actions their moral value. Since reason plays only a secondary role in the formation of moral ideas, it can only have an equally unobtrusive role in the science that explains them. As a matter of fact, this is not the only reason why the use of the experimental method in morality is necessary. Quite often—perhaps most of the time— we are ignorant not only of the distant goals of our behavior, but also of the real motives that govern it. Our action not only goes beyond the scope of consciousness by a sort of unexpected rebound, but also has its origin outside of consciousness. We act without knowing why; or the reasons we think we have are not the true ones. The heterogeneity of motives and goals, as Wundt has defined it, is no less important a truth because he has been able to formulate and establish it inductively.

Secondly, since moral phenomena vary with time and place, the academic socialists and the jurists of the historical school have had a certain tendency to view ethics more as an art than a science. According to them it is up to each age to see what suits it best and to construct its own morality; it is primarily a matter of practical ability on the part of a society and its leaders. They would probably not go so far as to deny that these facts could become material for science, but they have an instinctive dislike of general rules and categories. Schäffle had already rejected this notion. Wundt, in turn, shows that if moral ideas evolve, their evolution follows laws that science can determine, and he makes the determination of these laws the primary problem for ethics.

There is, however, one point where Wundt allows the idea that binds all these theories together to slip a little. We have seen that for all the moral theorists discussed here, the essential function of morality was to help people adapt to one another and thus to assure the equilibrium and the survival of the group. According to Wundt, however, morality only has this character in an unobtrusive way. It is, no doubt, a necessary condition of the existence of societies; but it happens unintentionally and as an aftereffect. The real object of morality is to make the individual feel that he or she is not the whole, but part of the whole, and to appreciate how insignificant he or she is by comparison with the expanse of the encompassing milieu. Since society is only one circle of this milieu—the most immediate one—a consequence of morality is to make society possible. But this is, in the final analysis, involuntary and fortuitous.

Morality is the result of efforts people make to find a lasting object to which to attach themselves and to experience a pleasure which will not be transitory. Once they look beyond themselves and have undertaken this quest, the first objects people meet are the family, the city, and the nation, and there they stop. Often, for that matter, these objects have no value in themselves but only in that they symbolize, in however imperfect a way, the ideals people seek. In a word, although society is one of the means by which moral sensitivity develops, morality creates society as a byproduct along with the instincts and tendencies that are necessary for it. This, however, is only one of the transitory phases through which morality passes, one of the forms it successively takes.

Given this account, however, one of the essential properties of morality becomes inexplicable: this is its obligatory force. Wundt recognizes this character in principle, but one must also say where morality gets such an authority and in whose name it commands. If one sees in morality a commandment that the divinity has given us, then it is in the name of God; if it consists of social discipline, then it is in the name of society. If it is neither of these, however, one cannot see whence morality can acquire the right to give orders. Can one say that it is only logical for the part to submit to the whole? Logic governs only the mind, not the will: the goal of action is not truth, but utility or the good. We are assured, certainly, that we will discover real worth in this obedience and that this should make us happy. This may be so, but concern solely for our happiness can never be the source of genuine imperatives. What is desirable is not necessarily obligatory. When we have acted contrary to our own interests, however important they might be, the regret we feel does not resemble remorse. We cannot obligate ourselves; every command supposes at least an eventual restraint and therefore a superior power capable of constraining us. A need or an aspiration, however, is just a part of the self and not normally detached from it.

Wundt furthermore recognizes two sorts of imperatives: those of constraint and those of liberty. But is it not clear that the two terms "imperative" and "liberty" clash when they are joined together. The former is evidently there only for reasons of symmetry; Wundt ultimately thinks that morality in its highest form is not obligatory.

Now it is certainly true that people with a high sense of morality submit to moral obligation without pain and even with joy; but this does not mean that they do not feel it or that it does not exist for them. Obligation, even when accepted with enthusiasm, is always obligation; a morality in which obligation is not more or less the dominant notion has never been found. So the question is raised again: to whom are we obligated? To ourselves? That is a play on words: what is a debt if we are at one and the same time the debtor and the creditor?

The idea at the base of this doctrine is surely not profound and could be accepted by even the most empirical moral theory. The fact is that we have a need to believe that our actions do not exhaust all their consequences in an instant, that they do not hold good only for the point of time and space in which they take place, but that their consequences are extended for some distance in duration and scope. Otherwise they would amount to very little; only a thin line would separate them from obscurity and they would hold no interest at all for us. Only actions that last are worth the trouble of being voluntary; only pleasures that last are worth the trouble of being desired. No doubt everyone does not feel the necessity of this in the same way. For the child and the primitive the future hardly extends beyond the next instant. The adult and the civilized person of an average education measures himself or herself in months and years; the superior person wants to have an even more extended perspective. All want to leave the present which they find to be too narrow. The prospect of obscurity is an intolerable punishment; and since it is always before us, the only means we have of escaping it is to live in the future.

None of our goals has an absolute value, not even happiness—as one Utilitarian has shown.[38] If they attract us, it is because we have faith in them by comparison with other things. If this were an error, if we were ever to perceive that behind these relative

---

38. See John Stuart Mill, *Memoires,* Ch. 5.

goals there was nothing but a void, the charm that draws us toward them would be broken and life would be deprived of meaning and attraction. If our efforts lead to nothing that lasts, they are useless; why should we labor in vain?

Furthermore, since individualism detaches the individual from everything, it confines one to oneself, closes every horizon, and leads straight to pessimism. What is personal pleasure which is so meager and short-lived? In fact, there is no better objection to utilitarian and individualistic morality. Just because human need is an important factor in the evolution of morality, is it therefore the essential factor? This does not seem to us to have been demonstrated at all. Could one not claim to the contrary that morality is above all a function of society and it is only by a fortunate coincidence that societies, since they endure infinitely longer than the individual, offer us a less ephemeral satisfaction? But Wundt asks why one should place such a high value on society. In part, because it serves our interests, but above all because it is the only realm in which our social inclinations can be satisfied, and these in turn are a product of the affinity which like has for like everywhere in nature.

What has led Wundt to his doctrine is his excessive denigration of the individual. But if the trees ought not to conceal the forest, neither must the forest conceal the trees. To be sure, Wundt acknowledges the great importance of individual effort; we know the place he gives to the influence of great people in the evolution of societies. But he seriously undervalues the very real pleasure we find in pursuing personal goals. If there is no happiness in the little things of life, there can be none in an abundance. If the immediate goals of action are without charm, the more distant goals would hardly attract us. One cannot take figures of speech literally. The joys that a person finds in himself or herself are limited and brief, but they are nonetheless positive; otherwise, however one expands or develops oneself, one's happiness would remain nil. In the end, Wundt only overcomes this pessimism by making it his point of departure. But if the life of the individual is not worth something, however little, then what remains is worth nothing and there is no remedy for this defect. If one puts a worm on a flower, one should expect to find it in the fruit.

Thus the happiness we are promised is full of misery! What is this endless course in pursuit of an ideal we can never attain but a long, painful and finally helpless effort to escape ourselves, to lose sight of reality, and at last to numb ourselves to the point of not feeling the misery of our meager destiny? I much prefer the words of the ancient sages who recommended above all complete and peaceful self-control. No doubt, for its continued development the mind needs to have more expanded horizons before it, but it remains finite and does not change its nature. This is why it becomes upset and confused by the notion of infinity. The sense of the unlimited has its grandeur, but it is painful and there is something morbid about it. We need to know where we are going, or at least that we are going somewhere. One can move the goal toward which we are inclined as far off as one wants, we must still be able to perceive it and must still from time to time be able to measure our progress toward it. If it recedes as fast as we advance, this would be like we were running in place. Is there anything more discouraging?

It is true that the Roman ideal was closer to the Romans than ours is to us. The ideal seems to move away as we move forward; but this is an optical illusion. Our current ideal is not the former one which has receded with time; it is a new one that has replaced the old as modern societies have replaced the Roman Empire. It will last as long as these societies last and it will vanish when they disappear, making way for other societies which will have other ideals. Certainly societies do not improvise on their own, they do not emerge abruptly out of nothingness; they rather rebuild with the debris left by the societies that have disappeared. The material they use is organized with a view to other goals, however; and we have no assurance that these goals will follow precedent or constitute a linear progression.

This touches on the postulate on which Wundt's method and theory are based. According to him there is *one* religious idea that successive religions throughout history have realized more and more clearly; *one* ethical ideal that has developed through all positive moralities; and *one* humanity of which particular societies are only provisional and symbolic incarnations. So to determine what this morality or this religion is, Wundt studies it in the relatively perfect forms which it attains among civilized people. Posed in this way the question allows only one solution. If all religions and all moralities are of one and the same species and pursue one and the same goal, this goal must recede as far as we approach it—unless one wants to admit that the day will come when life will stop since progress will be complete.

But if Wundt's conclusion is inescapable, this is not true of the premises. There are as many moralities as there are social types; those of inferior societies have just as much right to the title as those of cultured societies. Each nation, or at least each type of nation, has its goal which it approaches more or less until the time when another type takes its place and sets up a new goal. The goal toward which we move is not as infinite or as distant as it might appear. If our ideal today seems further away than it was at other times, this is because it requires more time and effort to realize it. If we see it less clearly, this is because it is more complex. It is no less definite because of this, however. The fault is in us, not in the nature of things.

Part IV

Conclusion

A. H. Post

Despite the divergent details which we have mentioned, there are some common traits among these doctrines which should be noted. Up until now all schools of ethics have practiced the same method: deduction. The only difference between intuitive ethics and what is called inductive ethics is that the former adopts an *a priori* truth as its principle, the latter a fact of experience. But for the one just as much as for the other, ethics consists in deducing from these premises, once they are posed, the consequences they entail. One begins from the notion of utility, the other from the concept of the good or of obligation; but it is just as apparent on the one side as on the other that the whole of ethics is encompassed in a simple idea and that it is necessary only to explicate this idea. "The intuitive school of morality," says Mill, "no less than what one might call the inductive school, insists on the necessity of general laws. The two schools have differences of opinion only concerning the evidence for ethical laws and of the source from which they draw their authority."[39] As

---

39. *Utilitarianism,* Ch. 1. [John Stuart Mill (1806–73, the most influential British philosopher of the century, was widely read in Europe. Durkheim was sufficiently appreciative of Mill's position to be occasionally labeled a utilitarian. He never denied the influence, but said that his critics missed the fact that he was even more of a Kantian (see Durkheim, *Contributions to L'Année Sociologique,* Yash Nandan, ed., New York: The Free Press, 1980, p. 138). Durkheim later continued to hold the view expressed here, that utilitarianism and Kantianism each emphasized an important aspect

to Spencer,[40] far from rejecting the deductive method, he criticizes
Utilitarianism for not following it closely enough. "In my opinion,"
he says in a now famous letter, "the object of ethical theory ought
to be to deduce from the laws of life and the conditions of existence
what sorts of actions necessarily tend to produce welfare and what
other sorts tend to produce misfortune."

The agreement between these two schools is even more complete. Although the principles which serve as the points of departure for their deductions may not be the same, they are obtained
by the same method. First, one cannot take the word of the rationalists and concede that they owe their fundamental postulate to
intuition alone. How could pure reason, without the aid of experience,
contain in itself a law to regulate domestic relations exactly, or
economic or social relations, etc.? As Secrétan[41] has rightly said, pure
reason would not even know that there are two sexes. So in reality
this supposed intuition amounts to a summation of the principle
facts of morality—a vague feeling for the elementary conditions of
the collective life. There is not one rationalist, moreover, who appeals
exclusively to intuition; they all recognize more or less implicitly that
it is not sufficient to say, 'Things are thus because this is how I
see them.' Rather, through a covert return to the same deductive
method which they formerly employed openly, they demonstrate that
it must necessarily be this way, and that logically the moral law
must be *a priori*, human beings inviolable, etc.

Their adversaries, on the other hand, proceed in no different

---

of morality and thus needed to be reconciled (see Durkheim, "The Determination of Moral Fact" in *Sociology and Philosophy,* Glencoe, Ill.: The Free
Press of Glencoe, 1953, p. 62).]

40. [Herbert Spencer (1820–1903), British sociologist, applied utilitarian
and evolutionary principles to the study of society. His empirical methodology
was a forerunner of modern inductive and comparative approaches. While
not heavily influenced by Spencer, Durkheim felt a definite affinity with his
concept of social institutions, his empirical orientation, his functional analysis,
and his view of the innate social nature of humanity.]

41. [Marc Louis François Secrétan (1809–1867), Swiss optician and Chris-
tian philosopher, wrote *The Philosophy of Liberty* (1849), *The Rights of Women*
(1888) and *Social Studies* (1889).]

a manner. If they say that utility is the sole end of our conduct, it is not because they have induced this general proposition from any methodical observation. They have not verified that in fact customs, legal regulations, or the maxims of popular morality have no other end. But, just as the others know instinctively that there is no ethical theory without a disinterested perspective, these theorists feel more or less clearly that it is impossible for us to act if we are not personally interested in our actions. They illustrate this point by a number of examples; then, to reinforce their thesis they make an appeal to rationality and logic and show that it would be absurd for people not to seek their own interests above all else. So the one school, like the other, bases its premises on incomplete and imprecise experience which they confirm later by means of an appeal to deductive reason.

But such a method, whatever conclusions one might draw from it, is not scientific. First, it has not been demonstrated at all that ethics can be reduced to a single rule and contained in a single concept. When one reflects on the prodigious complexity of moral facts, on this multitude of beliefs, customs and legal dispositions which increases daily, one cannot help but find that those formulas which are said to constitute the whole of ethics are really very simple and narrow. But let us say that there might actually be in the moral life a law more general than others, of which the others are only diverse forms or particular applications: in order to attain an understanding of this law it would still be necessary to follow the ordinary methods of the sciences. There is only one way to attain general knowledge: that is to observe the particulars, not superficially and all together, but minutely and in detail.

These comments apply as much to Mill as to Kant or Spencer. Despite the efforts he has made to rejuvenate Utilitarianism, Spencer has not given up posing his fundamental postulate in the utilitarian manner, which is to say that morality has for its object the advancement of the individual life, that the good and the useful are synonyms. That the principle of ethics might be such as he wishes is entirely possible; but it is really a question of knowing whether this is the principle of morality as it actually exists. Perhaps if Utilitarianism is right the moral life would be more logical and

more simple; but it is not the moral theorist's business to recon-
struct it any more than it is the physiologist's task to remake the
organism. He or she is only supposed to observe it and, if possible,
to explain it. At least it is in this way that one must begin; the
art of ethics must come later.

But even if one law were to dominate the whole of morality
and it were known to us, one could not deduce those particular
truths from it which are the substance of science. Deduction can
only be applied to things which are very simple, that is, very general.
Since these generalities are universal, the images which represent
them constantly recur. They are distinguished quite early from the
mass of other impressions and are strongly established in the mind.
They form its deepest layer, the unalterable base. The mind can
then act upon these kinds of objects without going outside of itself.
This is not true of complex things, that is, of concrete entities,
however. Since the representations which we have of complex things
are the latest to appear in the evolution of intelligence, they are
hardly more than rough sketches of things. The mind also forms
these somewhat as it wishes; this is why one can demonstrate so
easily what one believes or whatever one wants in these sorts of
matters.

Now moral phenomena are the most complex of all; the use
of deduction there is absolutely out of place. Surely Spencer has
reason to say that if certain types of conduct are better than others,
this is not accidental, and that "these results must be the necessary
consequences of other things." But in order to see how they are
produced it is necessary to follow the relationship of one cause
to another in reality. The link which connects ethical maxims to
the initial facts from which they are derived is itself a fact which
can only be known through observation and experimentation. Thus,
if we understand human nature and the nature of the physical
and social environment, can we then say how the former ought
to be adapted to the latter? Perhaps in some few simple cases;
but when the circumstances are the least bit complicated, reason
alone would be too weak in the face of the facts, and the theoretical
conclusion would stand a strong chance of not being the best. And
need it be mentioned that we are a long way from understand-

ing, even in an approximate way, human nature or the nature of society?

These theoretical observations were necessary to bring out the novelty of the German school. It is, in effect, a protest against the use of deduction in the moral sciences and an effort to introduce, finally, a genuinely inductive method. All of the moral theorists we have discussed are keenly aware of the narrow scope and artificiality of the ethical doctrines which thus far have divided people's opinions. The ethic of Kant seems to them no less insufficient than that of the Utilitarians. The Kantians make morality into a specific but transcendent fact which escapes scientific observation; the Utilitarians make it into a fact of experience, but one which is not specific. They reduce it to this confused notion of utility and see nothing in it but an applied psychology or sociology. Only the German theorists understand moral phenomena as facts which are at once empirical and *sui generis.*

Ethics is not an applied or derived science, but an autonomous one. It has its own object which it ought to study as the physician studies physical facts or as the biologist studies biological facts, and employing the same methods. Its facts are mores, customs, legal prescriptions, and economic phenomena insofar as they become the subject of legal dispositions. It observes, analyses, and compares these facts, progressively elevating itself toward discovery of the laws which explain them. It has, no doubt, certain relationships to psychology, since moral facts have their conditions in the hearts of individuals. But moral facts are distinguishable from psychological facts if only by their imperative form. Moral facts, furthermore, are related to all other social facts, but are not identical with these. Ethics is not a derivative or a corollary of sociology, but a social science beside and in the midst of the others.

Outside of Germany we know of only Leslie Stephen[42] who has followed this method and attempted to develop a true science of morality. This idea is the one which best characterizes the German school. To the names we have already mentioned we can even

---

42. [Leslie Stephen (1832–1904), British literary critic, wrote the *History of English Thought in the Eighteenth Century* (1876).]

add others. Lorenz von Stein,[43] in many of his works, asks jurists not to be content with commenting on the texts of laws, but to work for the development of a science which seeks, through the comparison of the laws of different nations, to infer the general laws of juridical phenomena. It is true that in an eclectic manner he maintains, beside this positive science, a philosophy of law which has the task of demonstrating the dignity of persons and the truth of the categorical imperative. But perhaps the science Stein calls for will be developed and organized and the philosophy will show itself to be unnecessary.[44]

Still it is incontestable that the practice of this method has had the effect of confirming some of the fundamental theses of evolutionism. There is not one of these moral theorists who does not recognize that moral ideas are the product of evolution. What constitutes both their originality and their superiority, however, is that the truths they claim are what they themselves induce from the direct study of moral phenomena, rather than being deduced from some plausible and undoubtedly most attractive hypothesis, which is nevertheless only a conjecture.

We would not even dream of contesting the principles of evolutionism; but it does not seem to us that one can base a science on it. Evolutionism is a directive idea, an idea in the back of one's mind; it is suggestive and fertile, but it is neither a method nor an axiom. A science has facts as its point of departure, not hypotheses. No doubt when a science is just being developed subjective opinions and conjectures constitute nearly all of it, and this is how it should be; but gradually as it consolidates and elevates itself, hypotheses shift from the bottom to the top. The evolutionary hypothesis has certainly rendered great service to the moral sciences; but all ought surely to wish that an ethic be developed,

---

43. [Lorenz Stein (1815–90), economist and political scientist, Professor at the University of Vienna, analyzed social issues of industrial society.]

44. See in addition to his *Staatswissenschaft*, Stuttgart, 1852, his book on the current status and the future of the science of law and political science in Germany (*Gegenwart und Zukunft der Rechts und Staatswissenschaft Deutschlands*, Stuttgart, 1876).

finally, which is neither spiritualist nor pantheist nor evolutionist, but quite simply a science of morals.

These hypotheses, moreover, have the fault of being formed by analogy; they are very general truths which are confirmed by a great number of psychological and biological facts which people now attempt to apply to ethics. Analogy is without doubt a useful instrument of discovery, but it has the major drawback of bringing into focus only the similarities which exist between things and of losing the distinctive features. So if one attempts to base the whole of ethics on a principle borrowed from biology or from psychology, one can be assured in advance of perceiving only those moral facts that are biological or psychological. In fact, this is what often happens to evolutionary theorists, especially in questions of moral pathology or, as it is called, criminology. It is well known, of course, that the criminologists of this school have a tendency to make heredity the unique factor in crime. They seem to forget that since these phenomena are moral they ought to be derived primarily from moral causes, that is, from social causes. No doubt in tracing the regression of causes one would end up meeting some psychological or organic facts; but if we focus upon these remote conditions of the moral life, we would thereby give up explaining what is most personal and characteristic about it. Morality ought therefore to be established as an independent science on its own basis, and this is what the German school is attempting to do.

But this method itself is in need of much improvement. The grave defect of all the works which we have analyzed so far is their extreme generality. Most of these moral theorists pose the same question as the spiritualists and Utilitarians, although it is true that they resolve it by a more scientific approach. They ask, straight off, what is the general formula of morality. Although they undertake to answer this question through an attentive observation of the facts, this manner of proceeding leaves morality in a situation which is quite exceptional among the other positive sciences. Neither physics, nor chemistry, nor physiology, nor psychology can be reduced to a single and unique problem; they consist rather of a multitude of particular problems which from day to day are becoming more specialized. No doubt the ultimate goal of the physiologist is to obtain knowledge of the nature of life while the goal of the psychologist is to obtain knowledge of the nature of consciousness; but the only way ever to obtain an adequate definition of either of these phenomena is to study in detail all of their particular forms, their nuances and varieties.

It is necessary to proceed in the same way with morality. The good, duty, and rights are not immediately given in experience. What we observe directly are particular goods, rights and duties. To discover a formula which will encompass them all it is first necessary to study each one in itself and for itself, rather than to grasp, all in one breath, a general definition of morality. Is there not really something strange in posing these high questions when we do not know yet, or at best understand only very poorly, what property rights are, or contract, or crime, or punishment, etc., etc.? Perhaps the time for synthesis will come some day, but it hardly seems to have arrived yet. Therefore, the moral theorist can only respond by an admission of ignorance, to the often repeated question, "What is, or better yet, what are, the ultimate principles of morality?"

So we must definitely renounce the idea of ethics as something commonplace and within reach of all minds. No doubt there is a common morality; there is really no other morality. But this morality is the object of science, not a science itself; it is not self-explanatory. There is still a world to explore where there are certainly some striking discoveries to be made. It is probably even easier to determine the laws of memory or digestion than to discover the causes of these complex ideas which were formed slowly over the course of centuries.

It would be quite unjust, however, to say that the Germans had not felt the need of introducing more specialization into ethics. All the doctrines which we have discussed, in fact, were transformed by the idea that the concepts to which ethics has been confined until now are abstract and empty because they are too far removed from the facts. We have noted that Wagner treats the questions he raises analytically, nor could we forget the passage in which Schffle recalls that there is not one virtue but many, not one duty but many. Moreover, the two final volumes of his work are given in part to an analysis of different laws and customs.

Although this idea is presented in all these works, however, it is rarely carried to its logical conclusion. Almost always the major preoccupation is to arrive at a formulation of the fundamental principle of morality. All the special studies we have noted are directly subordinated to this dominant question, and thus have something premature about them. One feels that they are not undertaken for themselves, but only to support the theory that is being proposed. The only German moral theorist who has been devoted to the study of the details on their own is Albert Hermann Post, who must now finally be mentioned.[45]

Post has a very curious and active mind. He started his studies of morality and the philosophy of law twenty years ago and has never abandoned pursuing his idea with a remarkable perseverance. Over time his views have changed. In 1867 he published a little brochure entitled *The Natural Law of Rights: Introduction to a Philosophy of Law on the Basis of Modern Empirical Science* (*Das Naturgesetz des Rechts. Einleitung in eine Philosophie des Rechts auf Grundlage der modernen empirischen Wissenschaft*) which was marked with the spirit of Kant and Schopenhauer. In his last work, however, he ends up an evolutionist. In the meantime he published a great number of works on the same subject: *Primitive Domestic Society and the Origins of Marriage* (*Die Geschlechts-genossenschaft der Urzeit und die Entstehung der Ehe*, 1875); *The Origin of Law* (*Der Ursprung des Rechts*, 1876); *The Origins of State and Legal Life* (*Die Anfänge des Staats- und Rechtslebens*, 1878); *Materials for a General Science of Law Based on Comparative Ethnology* (*Bausteine für eine allgemeine Rechts-Wissenschaft auf vergleichend ethnologischer Basis*, 2 vols., 1880–1881). Finally, the

---

45. [Albert Hermann Post, Justice of the Courts of Bremen, attempted to establish a jurisprudence on a historical and comparative basis. His aim, he said, was "to build up a universal science of law on the inductive method . . . to ascertain from the varying forms of ethical and jural consciousness of humanity in the customs of all nations of the earth, what the good and the right really are, and to establish in this circuitous manner what the real upshot is of my own moral and jural consciousness" (quoted in *Open Court*, Vol. 9, p. 4650. n.d.).]

work that we mentioned appeared in 1884: *The Fundamentals of Law and the General Traits of its Historical Development* (*Die Grundlagen des Rechts und die Grundzüge seiner Entwicklungsgechichte*). This book begins with some generalizations on law and custom which are not the best part of the work, and which occupy only a small place.[46] The rest is full of interesting facts and opinions. The author identifies the major juridical phenomena and traces their evolution in general terms. Unfortunately, this analysis can hardly be summarized, for it yields only a very small number of general conclusions. The author devotes himself almost entirely to recounting for us the successive transformations through which the law has passed.

The sociology of customs, however, ought not to be confused with the history of customs from which it draws its material. To describe the evolution of an idea or an institution is not to explain it. Even though we know the order of the phases through which it has passed, we still do not know its causes or its function. No doubt Post has in a way pointed out the reasons for the transformations he has described, but he can only do this in a hypothetical manner and without precision. To establish rigorously a causal relationship, one must be able to observe the phenomena among which the cause is presumed to obtain in different circumstances; one must be able to establish methodical comparisons. But one can only compare such phenomena if they are all brought together in a single field of consciousness and consequently situated on the same level. History makes all comparison impossible, since it places facts in a linear sequence and ranks them on different levels. Completely occupied with distinguishing phenomena from one another and with marking the place of each of them in time, the historian loses sight of what they have in common. He or she perceives only particular events and links them to one another; but by remaining with the particular, he or she does not achieve a scientific account.

The role of the moral theorist is to break these long chains

---

46. A. H. Post, *Die Grundlagen des Rechts und die Grundzüge seiner Entwicklungsgechichte*, 1884, pp. 1–30.

of phenomena, to bring links of the chain together even when they are separated by long intervals of time, to compare them and to extract their common characteristics. This is how one might make progress in discovering genuine laws in morality, that is, the causal relations between moral facts and the conditions on which they depend. Say, for example, that the question at issue is the right of property. Although it may have evolved in a unique way, still it might not be difficult to find a common basis among the various forms that it has taken. Moreover if one succeeds in determining from among the concurrent social facts those that have not changed very much, one would have the right to identify these as the conditions of the general characteristics of property rights. Or one might prefer to study a more special form, for example, the right to personal property; one would then have to observe which conditions vary at the same time and in the same degree as the right to property itself. We certainly do not mean to say that these problems are easy to resolve. Social facts are so complex that one will obtain nothing more than provisional hypotheses for a long time. But since they are derived from facts, they will at least have the value of objectivity and can be corrected and made more precise as the facts themselves become better known.

One thing more: it must be acknowledged that for the time being we are not in a position to apply this method to ethics with the rigor it requires. In fact, it is practically impossible to observe the form taken by things such as legal phenomena among all nations without exception. Then what can we do? Given the circumstances, we must confine ourselves to a few nations and disregard the rest; all our comparisons, however conscientious they might be, will necessarily fall short of a complete enumeration. The only remedy for this defect is to construct a classification of human societies. If societies were reduced to certain types, it would suffice to examine the phenomenon one wants to study in each type. Unfortunately, the historians, who ought to be giving us this classification, are not much interested in these questions. Entrenched in their own special studies, they most often refuse to venture beyond them. They repay with interest the contempt that philosophers for so long have heaped upon them and reject any alliance that they think may compromise their work. It is the theory of each for himself or herself, and everyone suffers.

Finally, the conclusion of this whole study is that the science of morality is only in the process of being born. We have recounted the persevering efforts our neighbors have made to establish it and have not underestimated the importance of these. One cannot deny, however, that a great deal remains to be done; this is an admission which costs us nothing. Perhaps the most important progress that psychology has made in the last twenty years has been to recognize that it is yet in its infancy. Morality can only gain by doing the same.

It will be said, of course, that there are practical interests involved here. Won't it shake people's moral beliefs if one asserts that they have such obscure causes? On the contrary, the conception of the sociology of morals that we have explained is the best safeguard for the traditional faith, since it shelters the traditional faith from its worst enemy, rationalism. If one thinks, in effect, that ethical concepts can be justified dialectically, that is the end of them. Since they are quite complex and the forms of logical argument are very simple, it will be easy to show that they are absurd. Some good and even great minds may take pride in having a hand in their destruction! But if one admits the principles described above, then one can tell young people, and everyone else, that our moral beliefs are the product of a long evolution, that they are the result of an endless succession of cautious steps, hard work, failures, and all sorts of experiences. We do not always perceive the causes that explain our moral beliefs because their origins are distant and so complex. Therefore we ought to treat them with respect, since we know that humanity, after such pain and labor, has not found anything better. We can be assured, for the same reasons, that we will find more wisdom accumulated in them than in the mind of the greatest genius. It would surely be childish to try to correct the results of human experience with our own limited judgment.

No doubt the day will come when the science of ethics will have advanced enough for theory to be able to regulate practice; but we are still far from that day, and in the meantime it is wisest to stay with the teachings of history. Morality would thus have quite enough authority in our minds since it would be presented to us as the summary and conclusion, however provisional, of human history.[47]

---

47. This essay was already placed with the publisher when we received a brochure by Wundt entitled *Zur Moral der litterarischen Kritik,* Leipzig, 1887. This is a very forceful reply to an article in the *Preussischen Jahrbcher* (March) on Wundt's *Ethik.* According to the passages cited by Wundt, one might ask whether the reviewer had seriously read the work of which he speaks.

GREAT BOOKS IN PHILOSOPHY PAPERBACK SERIES

ETHICS

SOCIAL AND POLITICAL PHILOSOPHY

GREAT MINDS PAPERBACK SERIES

ECONOMICS

RELIGION

SCIENCE

HISTORY

SOCIOLOGY

(Prices subject to change without notice.)